THE GOLDEN STATE OF FOOTBALL

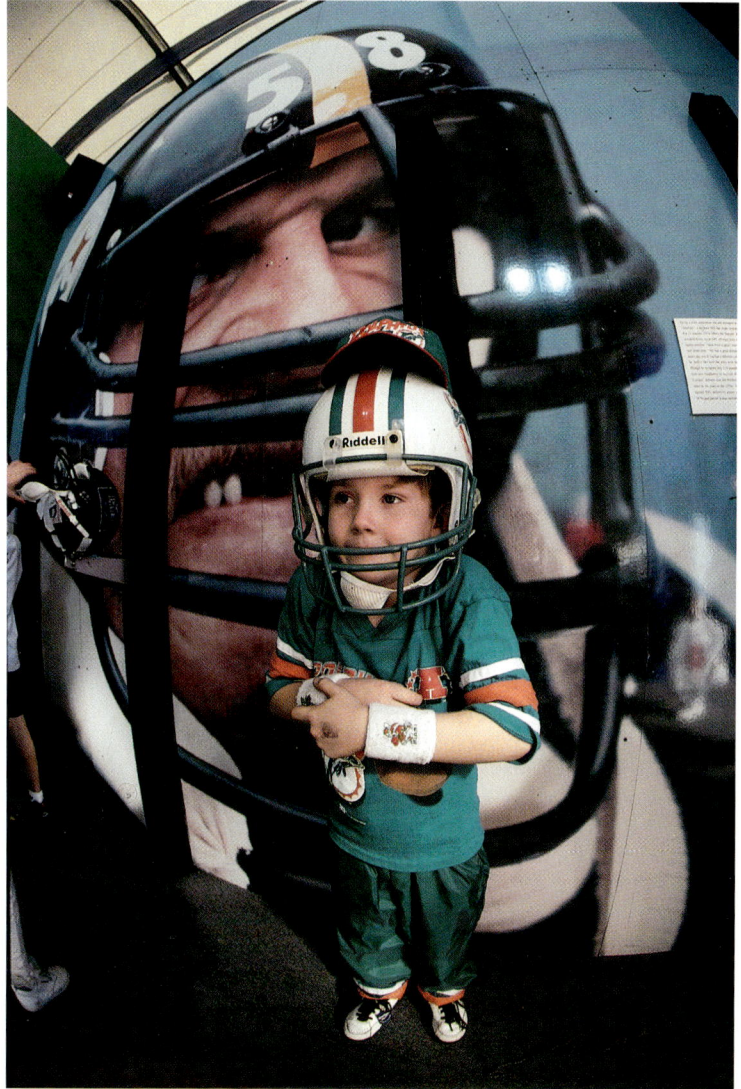

THE OFFICIAL BOOK OF
SUPER BOWL XXIX

THE GOLDEN STATE OF FOOTBALL

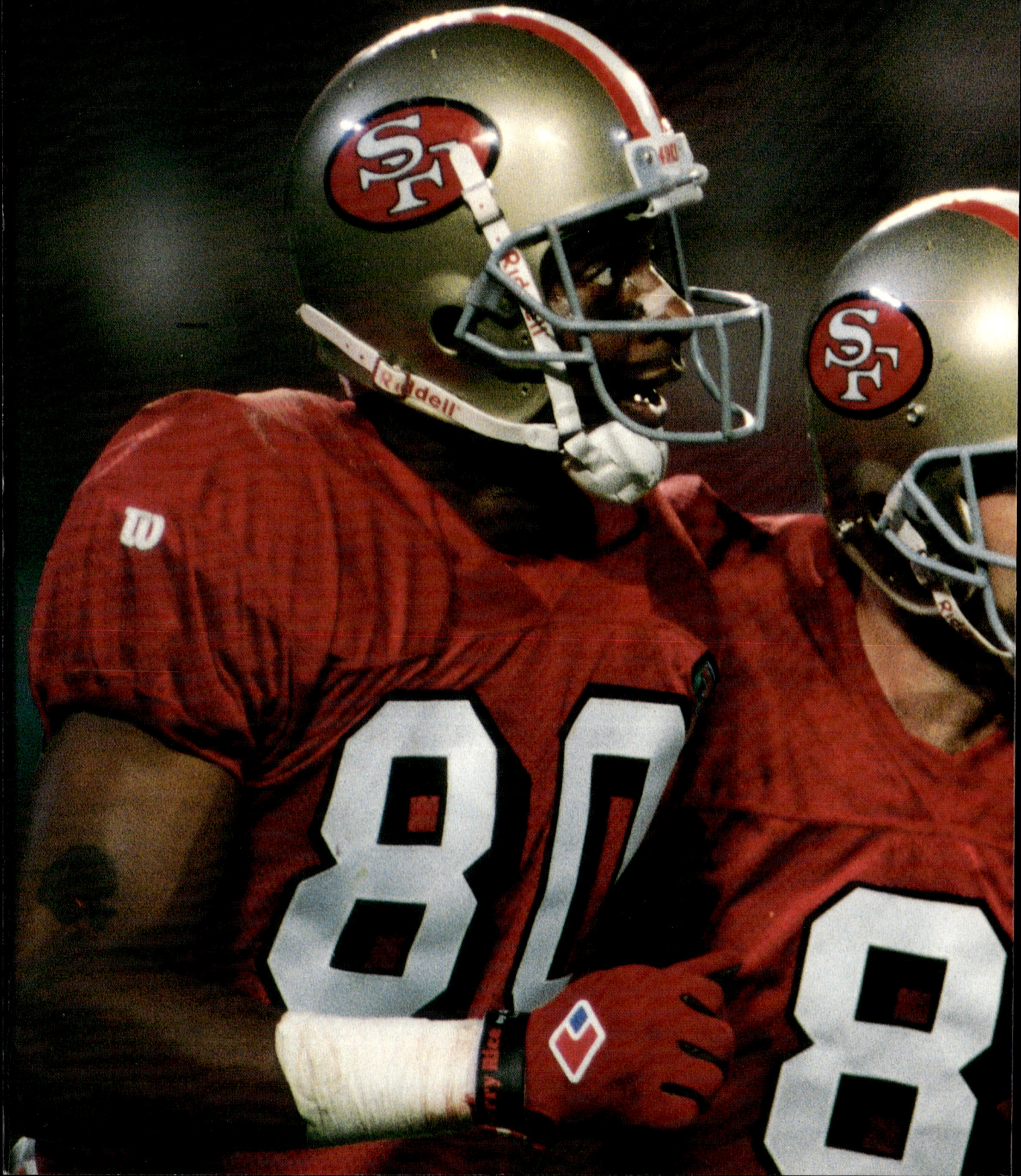

THE OFFICIAL BOOK OF
SUPER BOWL XXIX

WOODFORD PRESS
San Francisco

Designed by Laurence J. Hyman

Photography Editor: Dennis Desprois

Production Design: Jim Santore

PHOTOGRAPHERS
Rob Brown
Dennis Desprois
David Drapkin
Gerald Gallegos
David Gong
Stephen Green
Chris Hardy
Laurence J. Hyman
Allen Kee
David Lilienstein
Elizabeth Mangelsdorf
Al Messerschmidt
Fran Ortiz
Joe Patronite
Bob Rosato
George Rose
Manny Rubio
Jim Santore
Paul Spinelli
Sam Stone
John Storey
Kevin Terrell
Tony Tomsic
Baron Wolman
Michael Zagaris

WRITERS
John Crumpacker
Dan Fouts
Ronnie Lott
Jon Rochmis
Paul Tagliabue

WOODFORD PRESS
660 Market Street
San Francisco, California 94104

ISBN: 0-942627-25-3

Library of Congress Catalog Number: 95-60136

First Printing: March 1995

PRINTED AND BOUND IN THE UNITED STATES OF AMERICA

CONTENTS

THE OFFICIAL BOOK OF SUPER BOWL XXIX: The Golden State of Football was made possible with the support and assistance of:

Alameda Newspaper Group
Anderson's TV
Citibank
Contra Costa Daily Group
E. & J. Gallo Winery
Eastman Kodak Company
Escondido Times-Advocate
The Fan Club in San Jose
Flex-All

GTE
HOK Sport–Architects
KNBR 68–The Sports Leader
KTVU/Fox Channel 2
Modesto Bee
NFL Alumni-S.F. Chapter
San Francisco Examiner
San Mateo Times
Wheaties

FOREWORD

By Paul Tagliabue
Commissioner, National Football League

The National Football League's 75th anniversary season concluded with a dazzling display at Super Bowl XXIX, from the many community events during the week to the game that included a record 75 points scored. It was a fitting climax to a magnificent season.

In winning an unprecedented fifth Super Bowl championship, the San Francisco 49ers put on a show of football perfection that set a new standard in America's most popular sport.

Hundreds of millions of fans worldwide – the game was televised in a record 174 countries – marveled at the grit and precision of Steve Young, who set a Super Bowl record with six touchdown passes. They were captivated by the grace of Jerry Rice, who has caught more passes for more yards and more touchdowns than any other player in Super Bowl history. And they were impressed by all the other 49ers who contributed to the 35 Super Bowl records that were set or tied at Joe Robbie Stadium.

Like all champions, what set the 49ers apart was their teamwork. In the ultimate team game of football, the 49ers proved to be the ultimate team. It is a tribute to the leadership of Owner Eddie DeBartolo, President Carmen Policy and Coach George Seifert that the 49ers put aside individual goals in capturing the Vince Lombardi Trophy, symbolic of the best team in football.

The same is true of the San Diego Chargers, who advanced to their first Super Bowl, capping a 1994 season that was no less inspiring. Predicted by many to finish at the bottom of the AFC Western Division, the Chargers believed in themselves and the system established by Owner Alex Spanos, General Manager Bobby Beathard and Coach Bobby Ross. The final score of Super Bowl XXIX does not diminish the effort and accomplishment of Stan Humphries, Junior Seau and their teammates.

The Super Bowl is a celebration of what it means to be the best. I invite you to immerse yourself in that spirit within this book and to enjoy again and again a Super Bowl that will be remembered for many, many years.

THE CITY

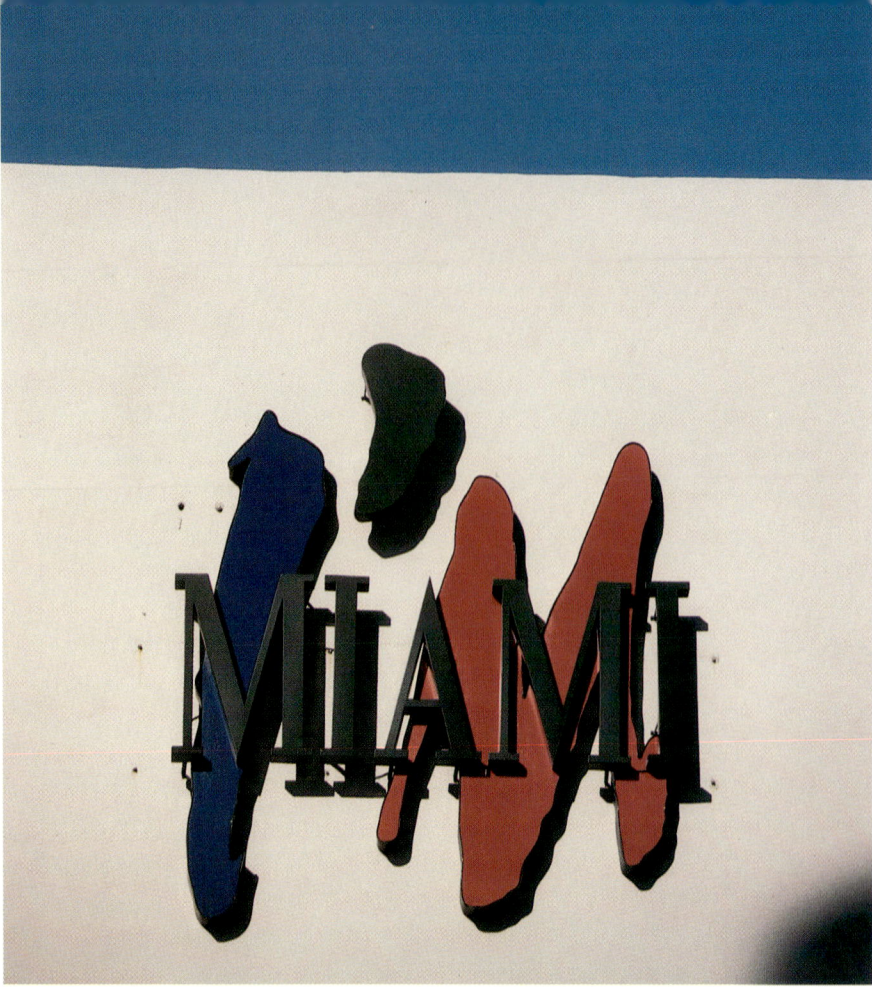

INTRODUCTION

By Dan Fouts

I was born and raised as a San Francisco 49er but I'm known in the football world as a San Diego Charger.

Needless to say, Super Bowl XXIX was special for me.

My father, Bob Fouts, was the "Voice of the Niners" on KSFO radio and Channel 5 in the 1950s and 1960s. That was a pretty good connection for a kid to have. I became the 49ers' training camp boy in the summer and their ball boy during the season. Had there been one, my job description would have read, "Must get in the way as much as possible."

I was a huge fan of the 49ers as a kid in the late 1950s and on into the mid-1960s. Those were pretty much mediocre days for the franchise; the team usually had records around the .500 mark, sometimes a little better, sometimes a little worse. But the games were fun and the players were great. I loved those guys: Leo Nomellini, Dave Wilcox, Bob St. Clair, Jimmy Johnson, John Brodie, Y.A. Tittle, Hugh McElhenny, Dave Parks, Charlie Krueger, R.C. Owens, Joe Perry. I could name them all for you. Luckily, I remain on a first-name basis with those guys.

Of course, they still call me "Danny."

In those days, like most football fans in an NFL city, I had nothing but contempt for the AFL. It wasn't a real league, an opinion not based on any rational thought whatsoever. The Raiders, across the bay in Oakland, were kind of a funny team. Their uniforms were adorned with silver numerals and they played wherever they could, at Kezar Stadium, Candlestick Park, Frank Youell Field. I remember going to Raiders games at Kezar thinking, "What a waste of time." It wasn't the Niners, so it wasn't real football. And football at Candlestick! This was long before the 49ers ever played there, and we thought, "How could they fit a football field in that place?"

That bias changed with one game, Super Bowl III. My first thought when the Jets upset the Colts was, "How could this happen?" But then I realized that the Jets were the better team, that they had played a better game. From that moment on in my mind, there was no difference between the two leagues. Joe Namath was a great quarterback in any league. Most football people agree it was really that game that validated the NFL-AFL merger of 1966, which made the league as strong as it is today.

There are quite a few similarities between the 49ers and Chargers, aside from the fact they're the first two California teams to play in the same Super Bowl, and both are in cities that are world-famous tourist destinations. The 49ers (All-America Football Conference) and the Chargers (in that contemptuous yet entertaining AFL) actually started out in leagues other than the NFL, and both were the first major league sports teams in their cities. For that reason, sports fans in both towns identify more with those teams than their other franchises. Also, Chargers and 49ers fans suffered a lot in the early years and then really became enthusiastic when their teams became successful on the field. And, of course, both teams are known for revolutionizing football on the offensive side of the ball.

The Chargers were struggling when I first got to San Diego in 1973. We didn't start winning consistently until my sixth season, and as a result, we didn't draw well until then. It wasn't unusual to see crowds of 25,000 at the stadium. San Diego State regularly drew twice as many people. Don Coryell had brought success to the Aztecs, and it wasn't until he came over to the Chargers that our great turnaround began.

A lot of people don't realize that Don was originally a running coach, but when he took over at San Diego State, he didn't have the personnel to go toe-to-toe with most teams. Luckily enough, Sid Gillman, the grandfather of the so-called "West Coast Offense," was running things across town with the Chargers, and Don spent a lot of time learning from Sid.

I was one who benefited greatly from those sessions.

The Chargers teams I played on never did make it to the Super Bowl. A lot of players who have had great careers and never made it to the Super Bowl say that created a void in their lives. I don't feel that way. Sure, I feel badly I didn't play in one, but there's no void. I had a good shot at it and I tried my best, as did my teammates. Plus, we were as memorable a football team as ever played the game. That means a lot. From 1978-1985, the San Diego Chargers were ranked No. 1 in passing in the NFL every year except one, and the only year we weren't ranked on top, we were No. 2. Nobody in the history of the league has been able to match that streak.

Naturally, the two most-often asked questions of me during Super Bowl XXIX week were: 1) Who are you rooting for?, and 2) Whose offense was greater, the 1981 San Diego Chargers or the 1994 San Francisco 49ers?

As a member of the media, my professional responsibilities preclude rooting. Plus, it's very difficult for me to sit in the press box. Football is such a hard game, and it just doesn't look hard from there. However, as I sat in my press box seat in the Joe Robbie Stadium end zone, I wanted so badly to stand up and cheer for both teams as they came out of the tunnel. I admit having deep emotions for both teams. But I knew my colleagues would give me a hard time, so I pressed the binoculars to my eyes and concentrated on the facial expressions of every player. It was still difficult to contain my emotions, especially when the Chargers came out. I felt a lot of appreciation for them, for what they did and how they did it, just to get to Miami.

To be truthful, I had to root for the team I played for. I just wish they had played better. The score was 49-26, but I think the 49ers could have scored 100.

As for the other question, I compiled a comparison chart, matching players position by position. Jerry Rice vs. Charlie Joiner, Rice has to get the nod. John Taylor vs. Wes Chandler, give it to Chandler. At tight end, Brent Jones vs. Kellen Winslow, I've got to go with Winslow. Fullback, it's William Floyd vs. John Cappelletti, advantage Floyd. At halfback, Ricky Watters vs. Chuck Muncie, and that's a push. So it's all tied up, and we move to the all-important quarterback position, Steve Young vs. Dan Fouts.

I think I'll pass on that.

Dan Fouts

THE CHA

™

MPIONS

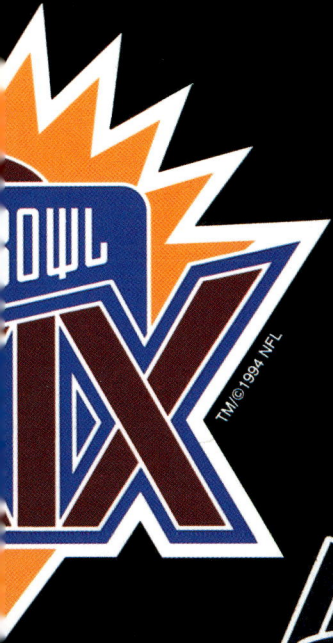

Chargers tackle Stan Brock visits with his parents as loyal fans give their team a heartfelt sendoff.

"The people of San Diego are euphoric right now."
—Bobby Ross

The Chargers, including defensive reserves John Parrella (left) and Doug Miller, embark on their well-deserved trip to South Florida.

"Everybody expected the Steelers to walk on in to the Super Bowl. After seeing San Diego go in there, with the 'Terrible Towels' waving in Three Rivers and making it to the Super Bowl, that's enough of a wake-up call that if it could happen to the Steelers, it could happen to us." —Ricky Watters

Eric Davis and Merton Hanks (above), Todd Kelly and Ricky Watters (top right) and Steve Young relax during a long week of plane rides and bus trips.

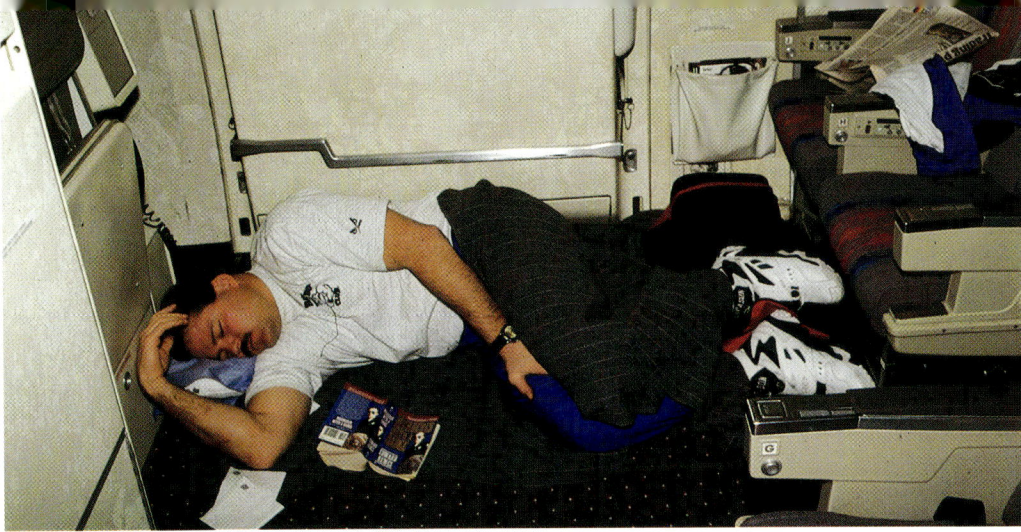

"There is no over-confidence right now. The only over-confidence might be in the media. As far as this team is concerned we are on a mission and it won't be complete until after this weekend."
—Ken Norton Jr.

Twelve-year veteran Gary Plummer's antidote for restlessness on a six-hour charter flight: a murder mystery and a place to stretch out; Ken Norton Jr., and teammates (right) disembark.

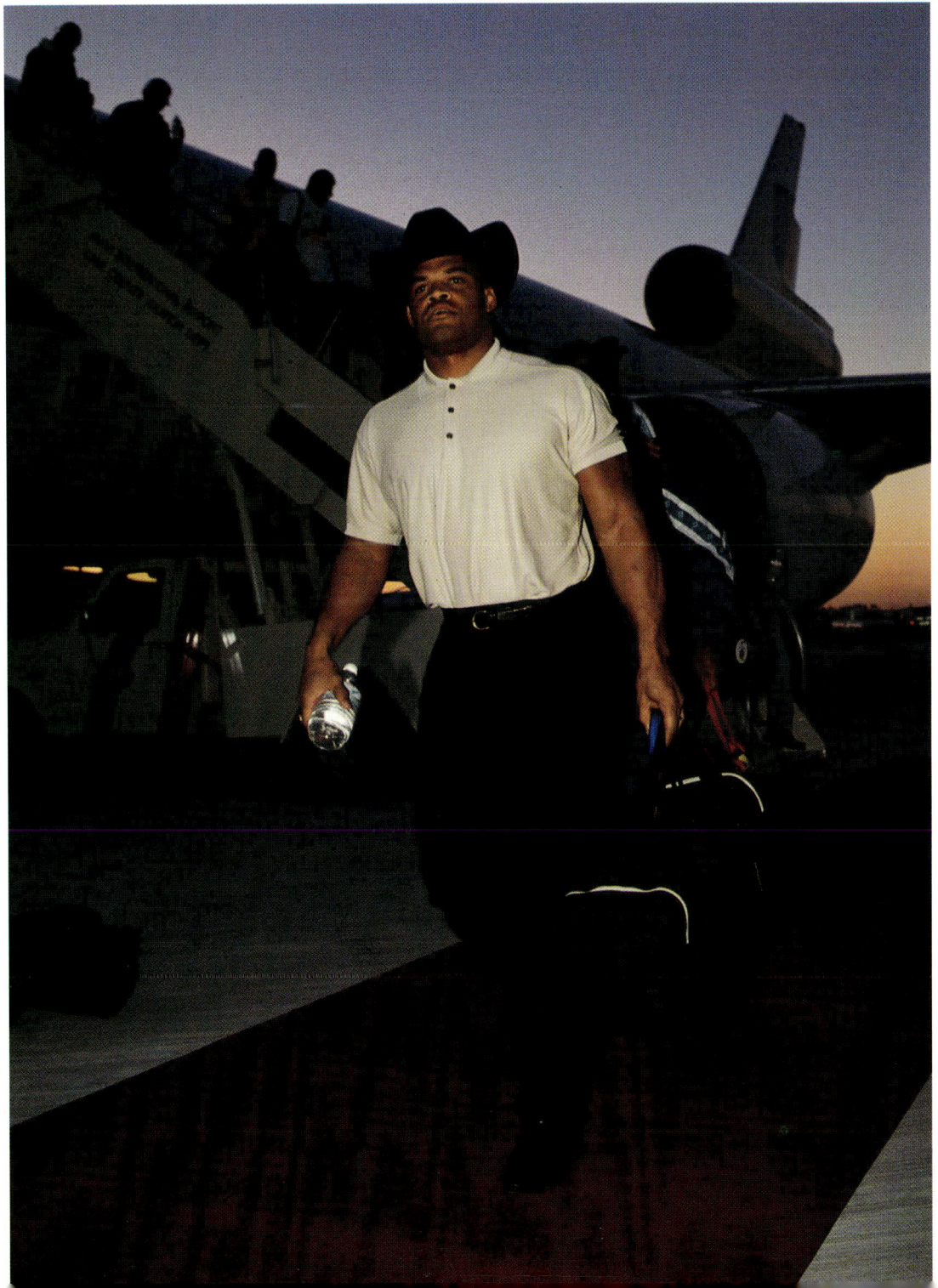

"He's kind of an old Western gambler, just a guy sitting at the table. He's not afraid to bluff. All of a sudden he'll go for the big pop. That's the way he plays football."
—Stan Brock on Stan Humphries

Media Day XXIX: Stan Humphries, Reuben Davis and Mark Seay draw big crowds. Right, the team assembles for a picture in the stands.

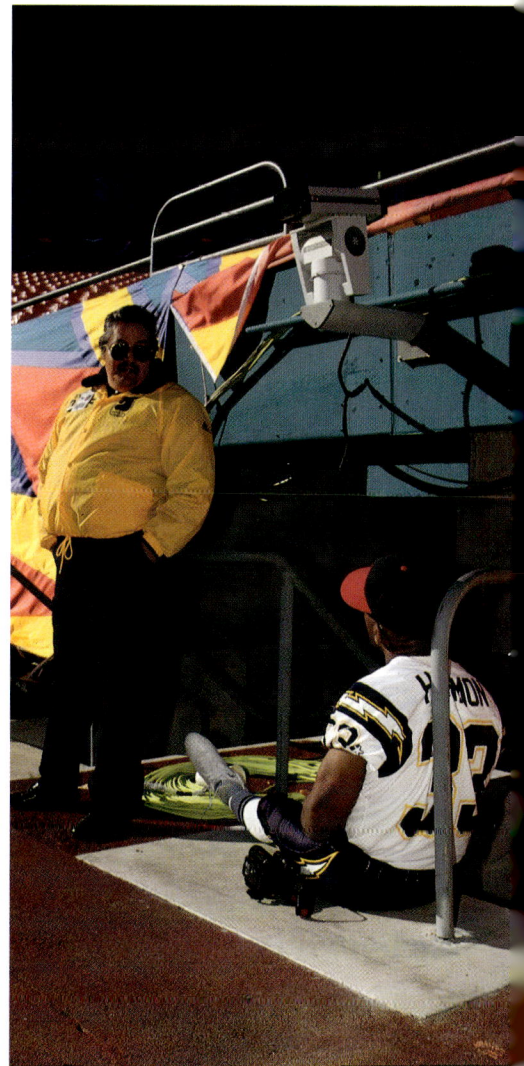

Natrone Means (top) and Junior Seau treat interview sessions seriously; General Manager Bobby Beathard and Ronnie Harmon find time for solitude.

"I think anybody who has played the game, from a kid on Day One, has wanted to play in the Super Bowl."
—Natrone Means

Going over the details at practice. Opposite, the defensive backfield turns its competitive spirit to a round of Rochambeau.

RICE

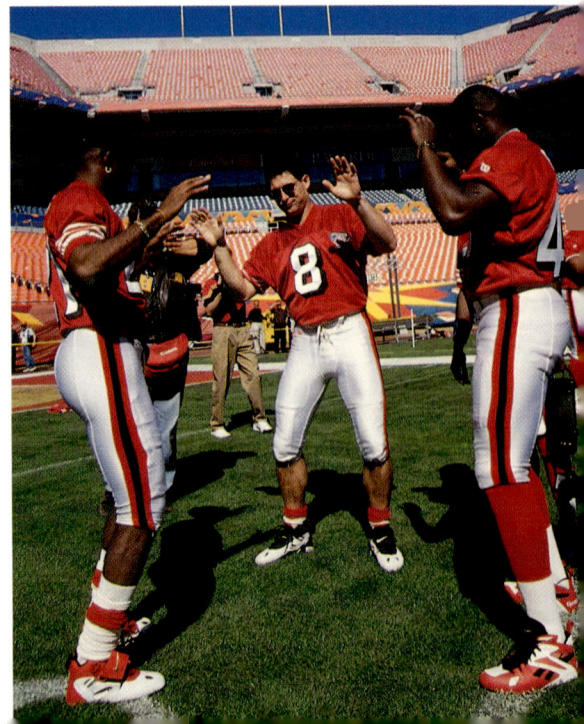

Jerry Rice draws a crowd, the team gathers for a picture and Steve Young learns the 'Prime Time' dance.

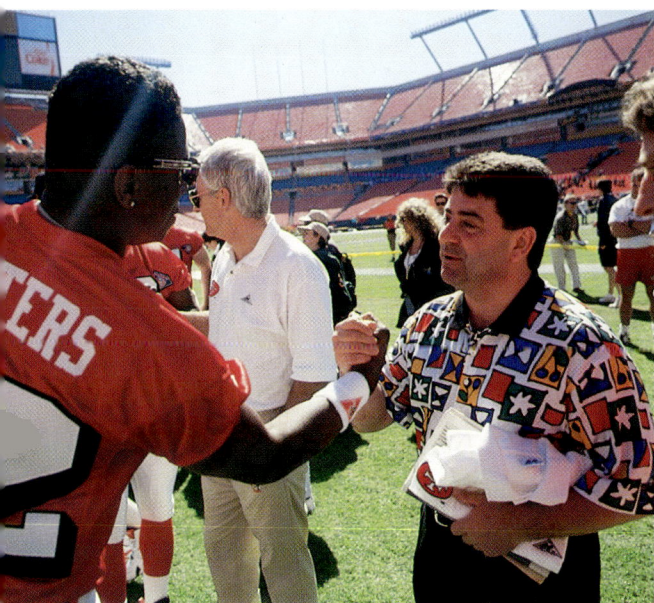

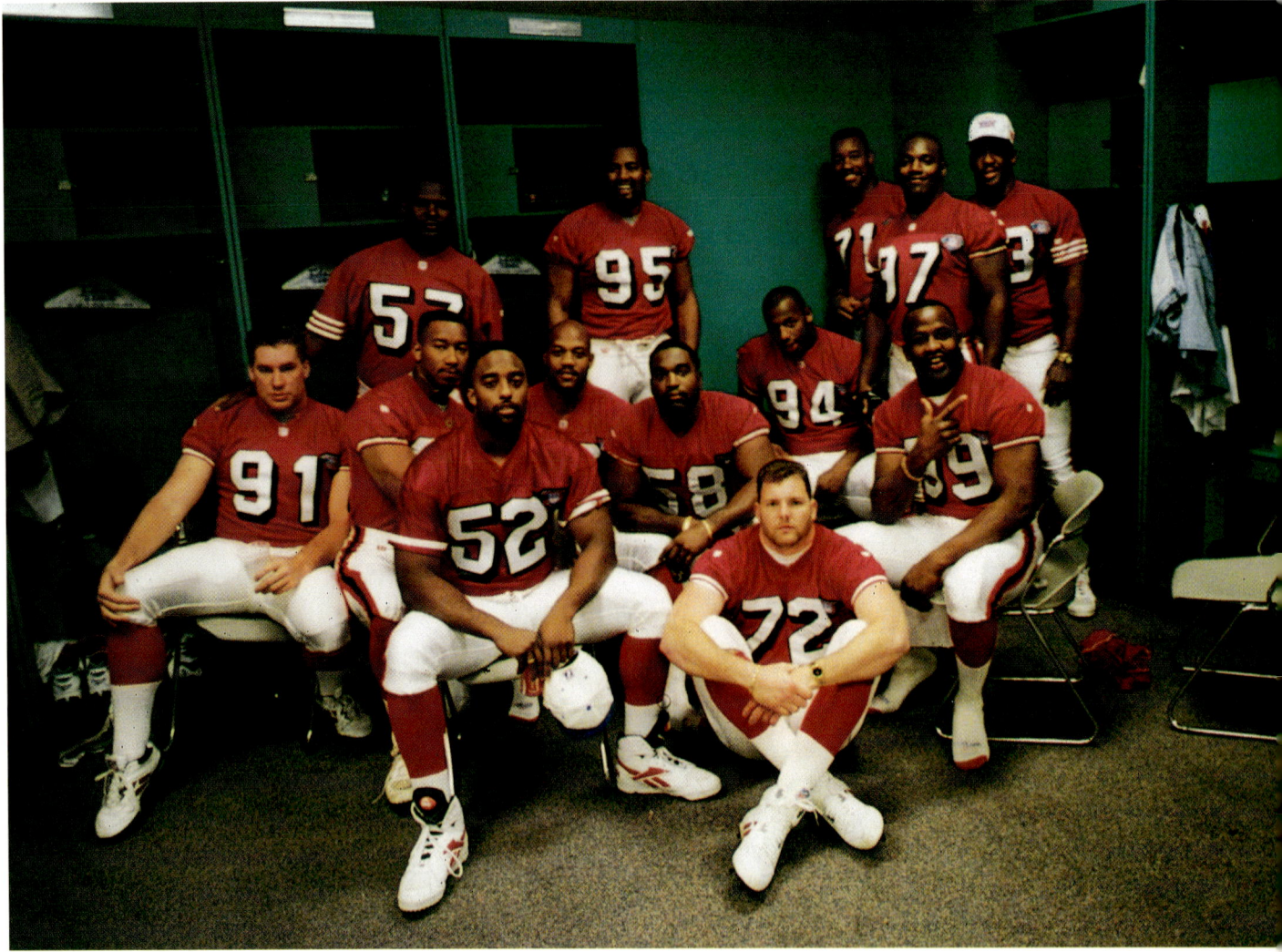

"The best way to get revenge is to be successful." — John Taylor

Top left and right, the pride of San Francisco and San Diego. Left, Deion Sanders shows off his Lamborghini Diablo, a $240,000 "gift to myself from myself." Above, John Taylor breaks a long-standing silence with the media.

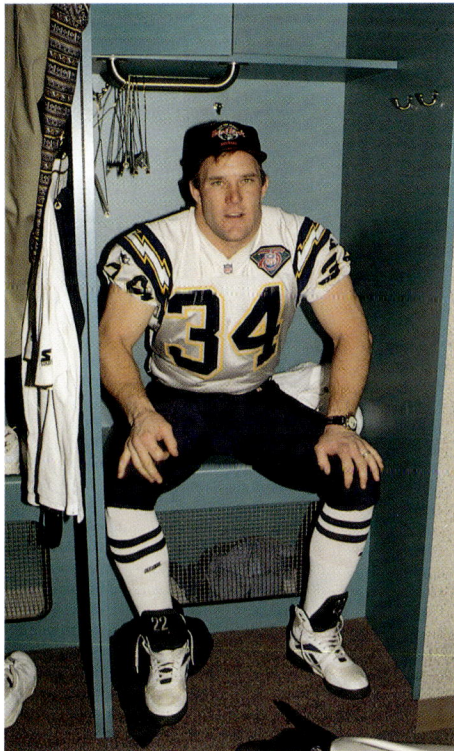

THE

EVENT

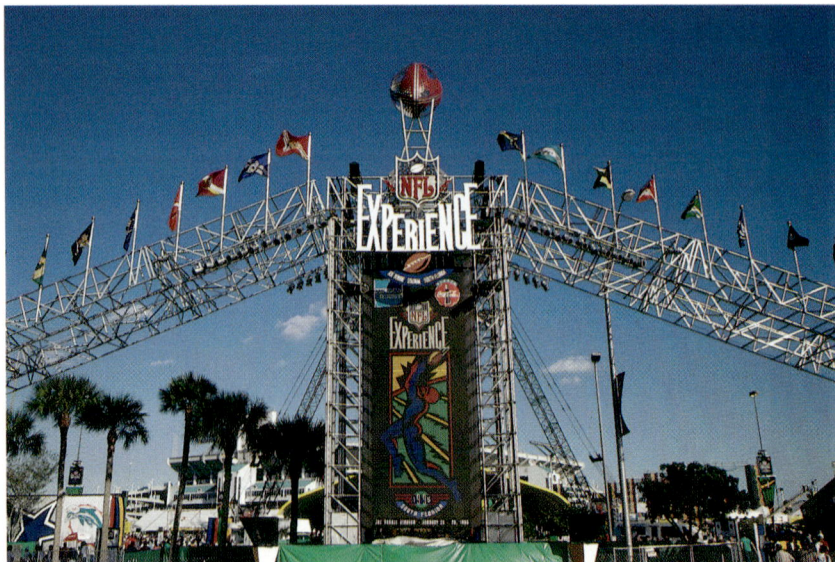

Teeming with activity, the grounds outside Joe Robbie Stadium provide the site for the increasingly popular NFL Experience.

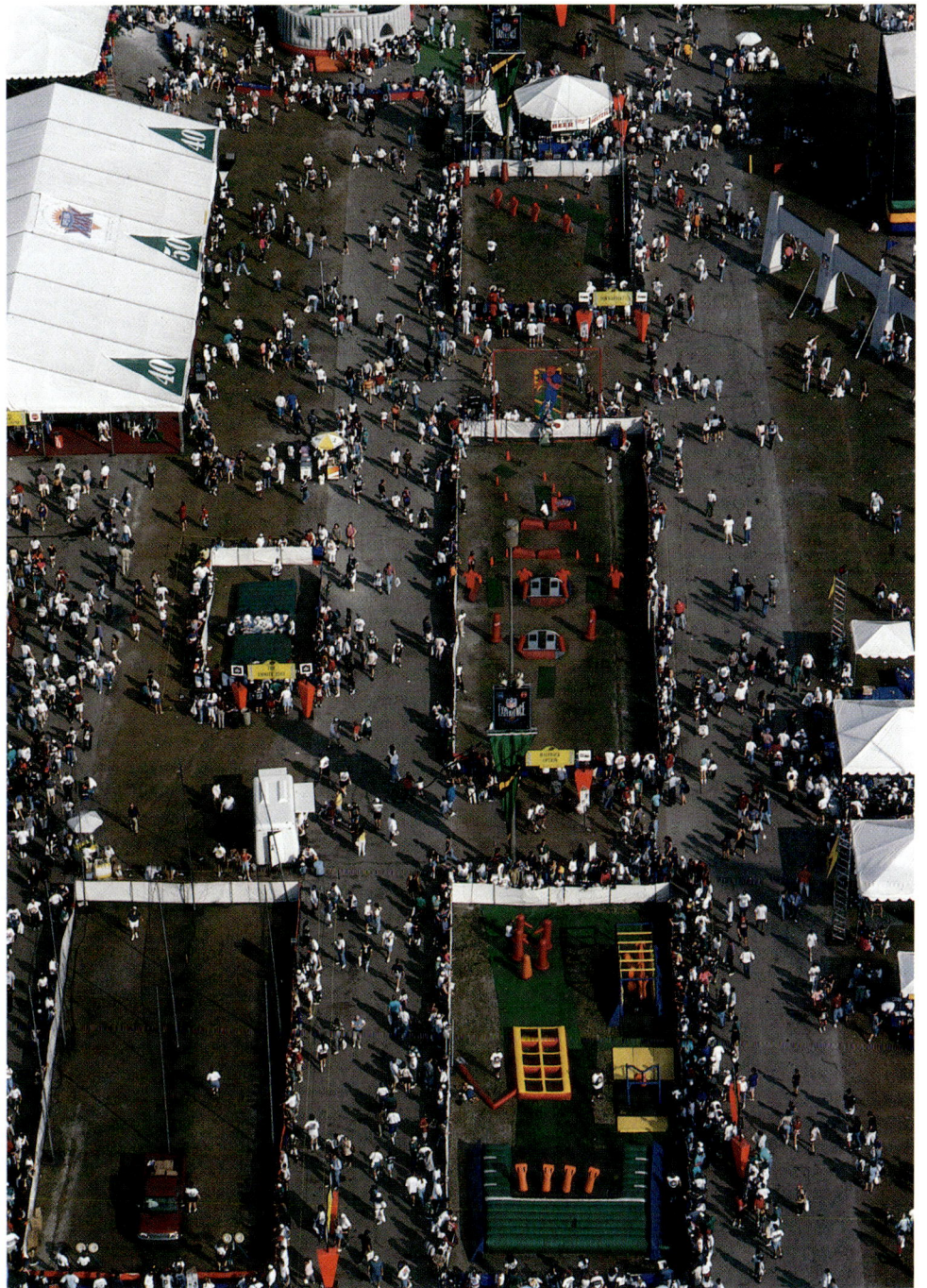

The NFL Experience is a place to play, learn, and even interact with such NFL stars as Neil O'Donnell (opposite, bottom left).

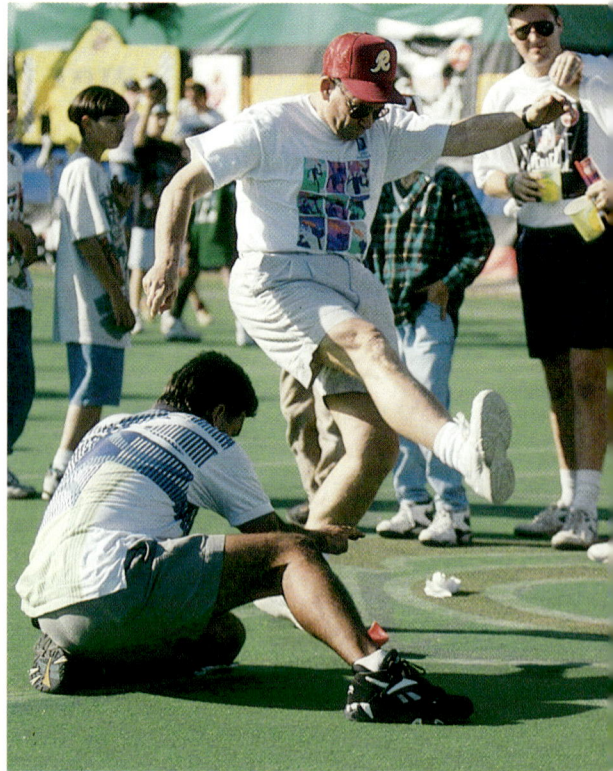

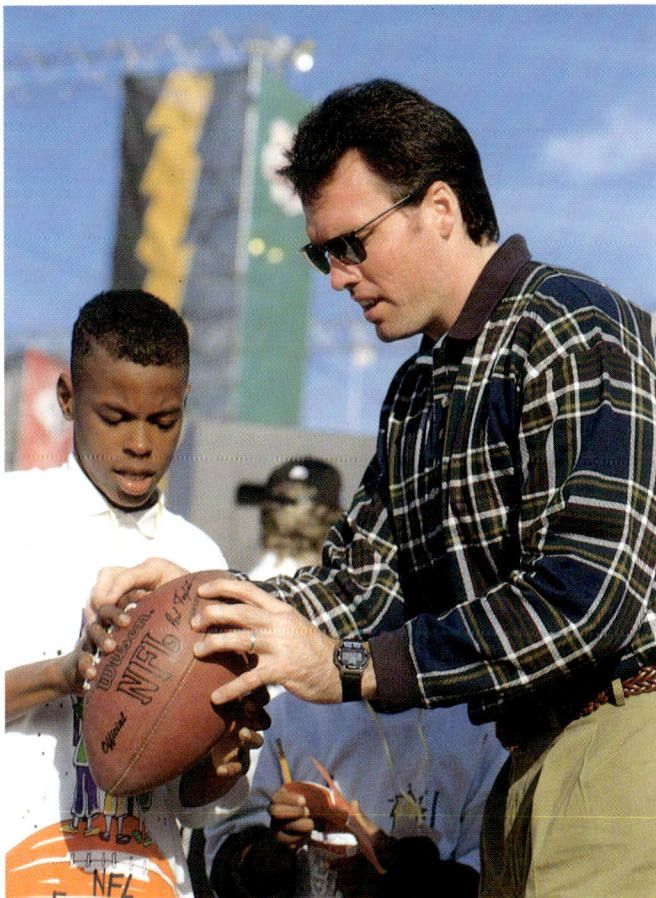

"My mom said we could go to Disney World or here."   —Richard F., 11, Greenville, S.C.

All athletic skills are represented at the multi-faceted NFL Experience, but nobody is in danger of getting a big head.

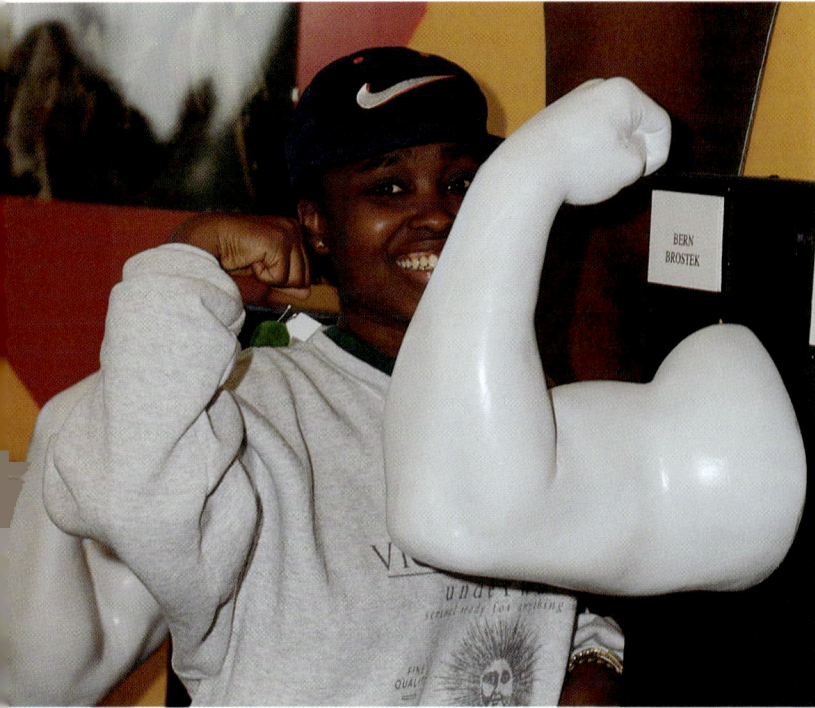

The NFL Experience brings fans as close as an arm's length away from the game. Opposite, bottom right, Seattle Seahawks defensive standout Cortez Kennedy shows his appreciation for his young fans.

"The best part was meeting the real NFL players." —Amanda H., 9, Athens, Ga.

ATTENTION
PLEASE KEEP OFF FIELD

WE HAVE SOME NEW ADDITIONS TO OUR GRASS FAMILY QUIETLY GROWING.

THEY NEED PEACE AND QUIET AS YOU KNOW, GRASS GROWS BY INCHES, AND IS KILLED BY FEET.

The entire NFL Groundcrew appreciates your cooperation

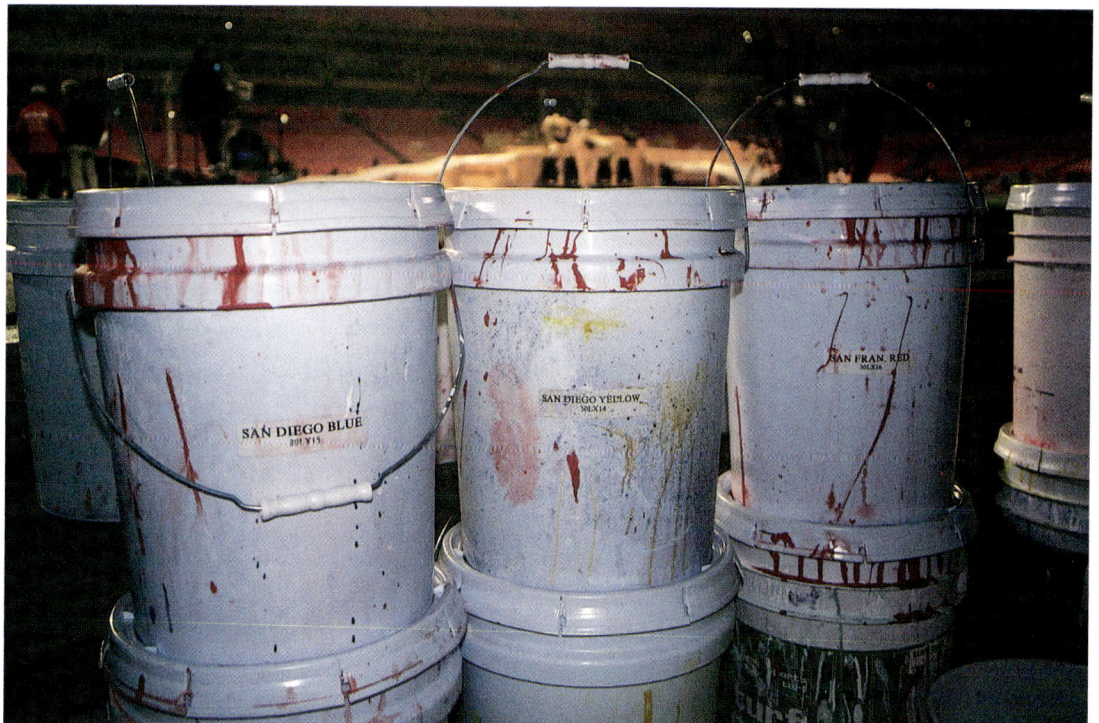

Opposite top, Detroit Lions star Lomas Brown displays the proper mechanics of the three-point stance. Meanwhile, inside the stadium, groundskeepers prepare the field (this page) and performers perfect their routines (following pages) as game day approaches.

"I can't believe I am here at the Super Bowl. I want it to last forever, but at the same time, I can't wait to play the game."   —Andre Coleman

A MODERN-DAY RITUAL

By John Crumpacker

The Rome of 2,000 years ago can be seen in the Rome of today, most noticeably in the Colosseum preserved in its perpetual decay and in Circus Maximus where chariots once raced, leaving a legacy for the ages.

If American cities of today were similarly advanced 2,000 years, would scholars find signs of ritual games in the compressed geometry of ruined stadia? Well, yes, but assuming videotapes preserve well, excavation and exploration won't be necessary. Historians will readily see what happened when tens of thousands of people gathered for games of competition and, yes, corporate gamesmanship.

The Super Bowl that came in a week and left in a Miami minute – actually, the 84 seconds it took the San Francisco 49ers to score their first touchdown in a 49-26 ritual slaughter of the San Diego Chargers – will be noted as much for the spectacle it provided as the sport it showcased. The great tenor Luciano Pavarotti sang, as did the great honorary San Franciscan, Tony Bennett, man of 1,000 hearts, none of them left in Miami. Other entertainers were invited to perform for the estimated 120,000 visitors to South Florida during Super Bowl week. Kathie Lee Gifford sang the National Anthem while her husband, Frank, sang the praises of the 49ers on national television . . . and why is it the National Anthem is sung most often at sporting events delineated sharply by city boundaries? It is a curious dichotomy driven by a fleeting sense of unity and a promise of mayhem.

The Super Bowl unites past with present better than any other sporting event in that it is one game held in one city and celebrated beforehand for one week. The Olympics, majestic as they are in their historical linkage, are too vast for the waning attention span of a people attuned to instant gratification. The World Series and NBA Championships likewise stretch out a little too long in their serves and volleys between two cities.

The Super Bowl is unique in that it takes six months to decide the combatants, two weeks to celebrate and three hours to resolve. It is truly America's secular holiday, weaving serpentine around a fragmented and often polarized populace with forked tongue testing the air for suitable prey. The Super Bowl is, in fact, global, but reports of the game being shown from Antarctica to Antigua are mere sidebars, as in eavesdropping on foreign TV announcers calling the game back home and wondering, "Hey, how do you say 'encroachment' in Japanese?"

Unlike soccer's World Cup, which America hosted in 1994, the Super Bowl is an American creation with the rest of the world allowed to watch.

It took the Super Bowl exactly three years to grow in stature from the AFL-NFL Championship to a day of national celebration. Joe Namath and his New York Jets elevated the game to an annual rite of smashage in 1969 with their upset of the monumentally favored Baltimore Colts. One can imagine an upset in ancient Rome having the same effect on the old empire: "Underdog Christian Stuns Roman; Money Lenders in Panic."

It has been with us long enough now to forget the Super Bowl's direct link to ancient Rome. Is it mere coincidence that each game has come to be identified by its Roman numerals? It wasn't enough to say Super Bowl 5 or Super Bowl 11 (not to be confused with II) or Super Bowl 29, the most recent one. No, it had to be V and XI and XXIX. And who among the crowd of spectators at Joe Robbie Stadium would not say that the players are not merely players but gladiators after seeing them bound up in plastic armor? Baseball is a game played in caps. Basketball is a game played in shorts and sneakers. Football, if it's not war, then is at least its ritual cousin, once removed.

"To be there for the National Anthem, to see the way they turned the lights down, to know that millions and millions of people were going to watch the game, it made me teary-eyed before the game," said Tim McDonald, the 49ers' strong safety and a man not observed to be teary-eyed all season.

Some battles are long and bloody, others are brief skirmishes. Super Bowl XXIX was decided, quickly and repeatedly, in the air, as modern technological warfare usually is. San Francisco had superior talent at the fleet positions in Jerry Rice and Ricky Watters and the best man to send them on their way, the virtuous left-hander, Steve Young. It was over at halftime, a time of still more rituals – mainly, restocking larders of food and drink – while singers sang, dancers danced and musicians made music that could not be heard behind the bulletproof glass of the press box.

In Miami, the game was heralded on land, on sea and in the air. Fireworks exploded over the water at Miami Beach as celebrants huddled by massive bonfires in the sand to stave off unexpected cold early in the week. At a Tuesday party, players from both teams melted in with milling civilians at an outdoor party and made a processional march on the various food stations. The Super

Bowl as secular religion is observed by consuming vast amounts of food that do not require silverware to make piecemeal. Bacchus would be proud, too, at the libations poured down the throats of revelers.

The theory of the Super Bowl seems to be, let's throw a party and end it with a game, much as the ancient Romans did with their competitions – minus the information superhighway.

The day of the game began early for the revelers and ended late for the legions of scribes, an ancient term for that low profession almost as old as old Rome itself. More than 2,600 people representing wide-ranging conduits of information services were given credentials to cover Super Bowl XXIX. Most media members went about the week with a weary sense of purpose, some took a lighthearted approach and still others pitched their tents in the Campground of the Insipid. A woman with a microphone went around asking players what kind of underwear they favored – briefs or boxers – apparently not aware of a third option: "None, ma'am." Harry Boatswain, a 295-pound lineman for the 49ers, created his own photo-op by bench-pressing the woman, to the hoots and hollers of his mates. Then there was the TV fellow who took the measure of San Diego wide receiver Mark Seay and blasted, staccato-like, "Mark, the shooting in 25 words or less!" To his credit, Seay did not rise up and smote this wandering infidel bent on trivializing a 1988 event that could have cost the young man his life as he shielded his three-year-old niece from urban harm.

While it is easy for cynics to cast stones at the glass house of the Super Bowl for all its excesses, the essence of the game is still about the skill and precision of the teams and the pride, passion and pathos of the players. San Francisco tackle Harris Barton wrote the name of his late father on his right glove, in honor of the man who died in May of brain cancer. This one's for you, Paul C. Barton. San Francisco players Rickey Jackson and Deion Sanders spent some of their free time brightening the lives of their mothers, who live in the respective Florida towns of Pahokee and Ft. Myers. San Francisco quarterback Steve Young chased away the shadow – if not the legend itself – of Joe Montana, and collapsed afterward from dehydration, proving that emotion is as much a fluid as the sweat of a man's effort.

"We set ourselves up for either the greatest success or a horrible failure," Young said. "I'm really happy we played our best football in the Super Bowl. That's our biggest relief and point of pride, that we played our best in January. Maybe some of the best football that's ever been played."

In the end the 49ers won easily because of what is arguably the best offense in league history, one that pumped out nearly 32 points per game. San Francisco's coach, the seemingly grim metronome George Seifert, was baptized with the gratuitous bucket of ice water. And a lustrous silver trophy named in honor of the late Vince Lombardi was given away by Commissioner Paul Tagliabue. The first person to deposit his fingerprints on the gleaming trophy was 49ers Owner Eddie DeBartolo Jr., who said above the din, "This is a very, very important victory." His father, Edward Sr., had died of pneumonia a month before the game. This one's for you, too, Edward DeBartolo Sr.

After the game various 49ers posed for pictures with the trophy that went from February to June in the planning and July to January in the playing. "It's pretty phenomenal," 49ers rookie linebacker Lee Woodall said. "I'm very over-whelmed. It actually hit me. I know this is a dream that's true. It's reality."

DeBartolo received the traditional congratulatory phone call from President Clinton, recalling if not repeating the ancient practice of politicians welcoming their conquering heroes of wars and games, if any was the difference 2,000 years ago. Past is prologue, but these days at least, no one is killed for losing. Never mind the hyperbolic words of 49ers President Carmen Policy, who said before the game, "What happens if we lose? We die." Both teams left the field alive and returned to their sponsoring cities nearly 3,000 miles to the west where they were greeted by massive, heartfelt victory parades.

"I feel very blessed to stand here on top of the mountain, arms held high, not once, not twice, but three times," said 49ers linebacker Ken Norton Jr., the first player to win three straight Super Bowl championships, the first two with Dallas.

Although the trappings of the game sometimes challenge the limits of pomp and ceremony, players on both sides are just as often overcome with the wonder of the moment.

As a ritual link to a shared past, the Super Bowl holds, with resolute strength, its position in the chain of history.

PREGAME

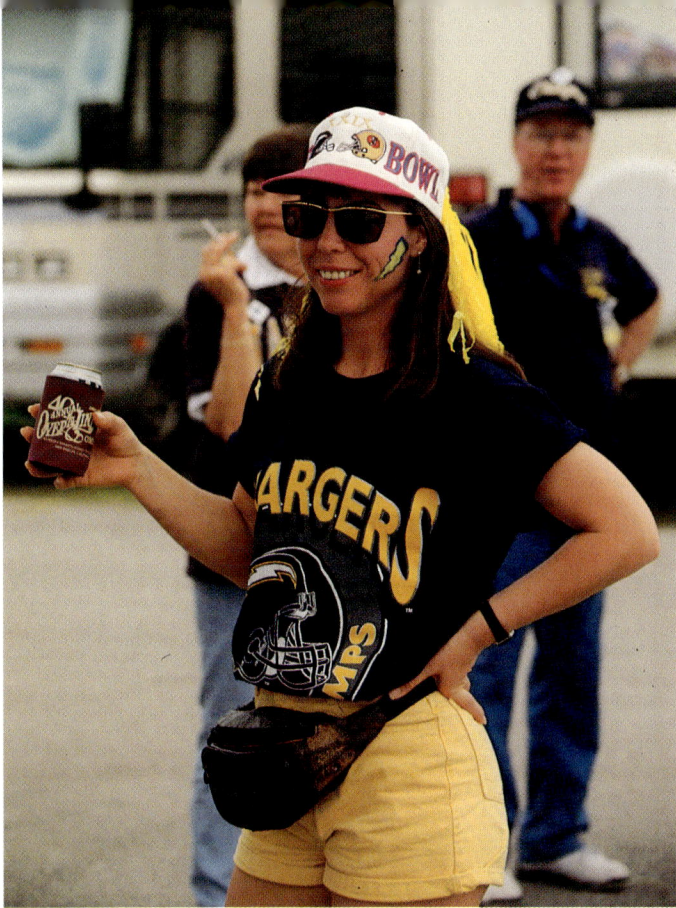

Outside Joe Robbie Stadium, it's not difficult to determine team allegiances.

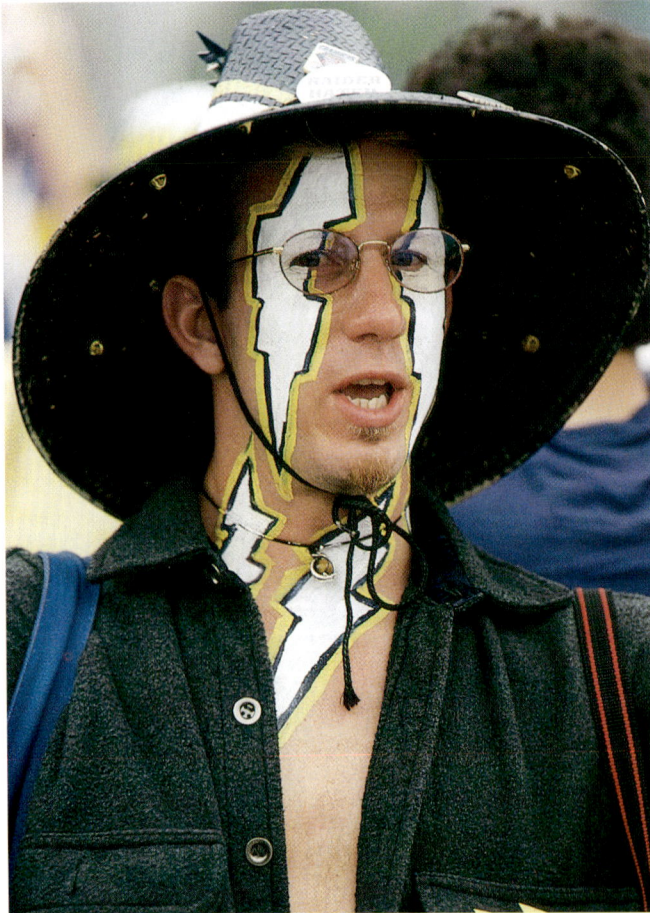

Fans with and without tickets flock to Joe
Robbie Stadium as gametime approaches. So
do league VIPs such as Raiders Owner Al Davis.

The look and texture of the Joe Robbie Stadium bowl changes dramatically as the fans settle into their seats and day turns to night.

The Chargers loosen up in a variety of ways:
Bryan Wagner works on a crossword puzzle;
Stan Humphries and Gale Gilbert skim the Super
Bowl XXIX Program; others stretch.

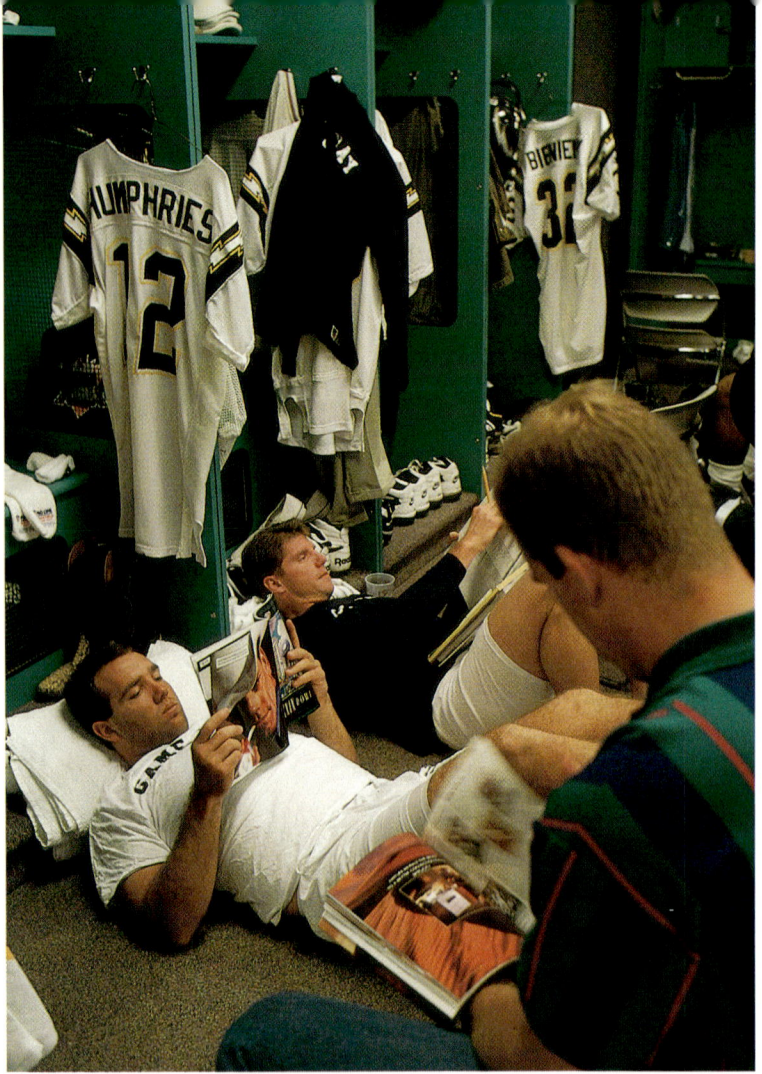

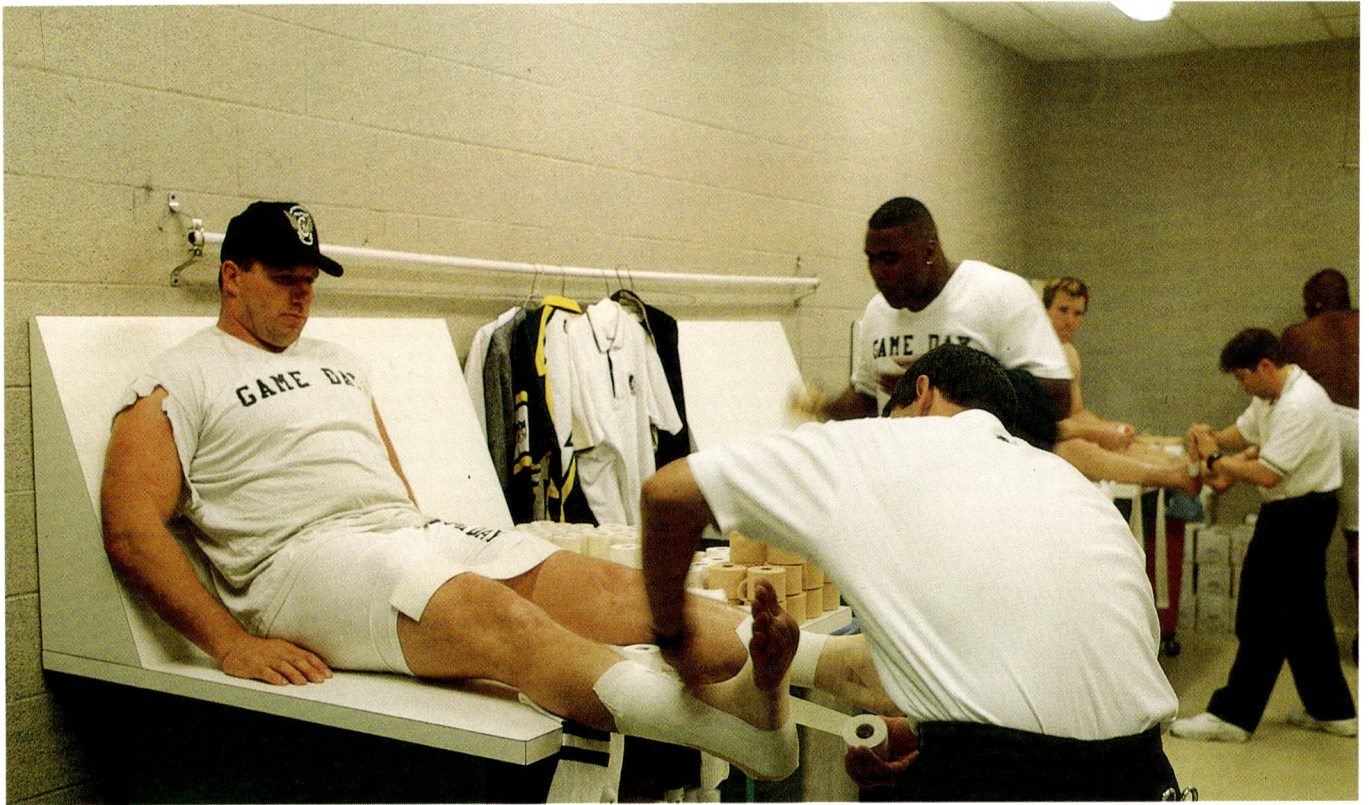

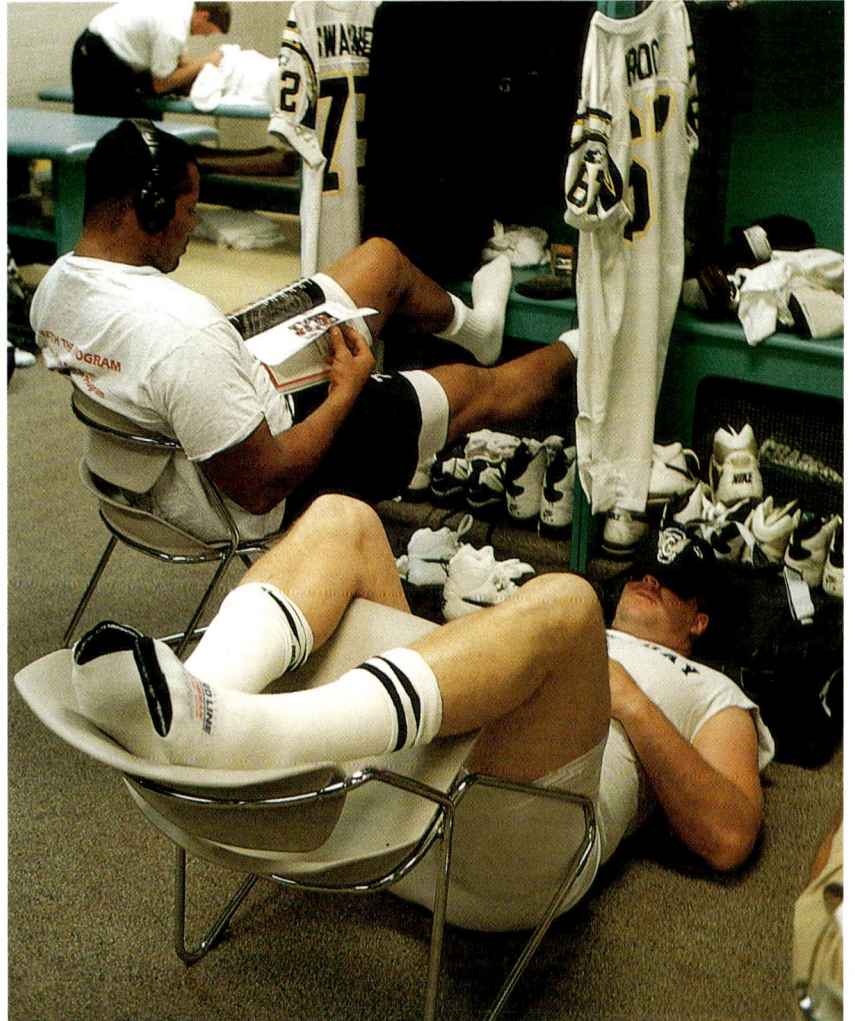

After getting his legs taped (top), Stan Brock takes a nap next to Harry Swayne (right). Above, Andre Coleman.

"Maybe we're just a blue-collar team. If we had commercials, we'd probably be selling ratchet wrenches." —Darren Carrington

49ers Lee Woodall and Derek Loville, stadium entertainers,
fans of both teams and off-site vendors, enjoy the
camaraderie and spirit of the game.

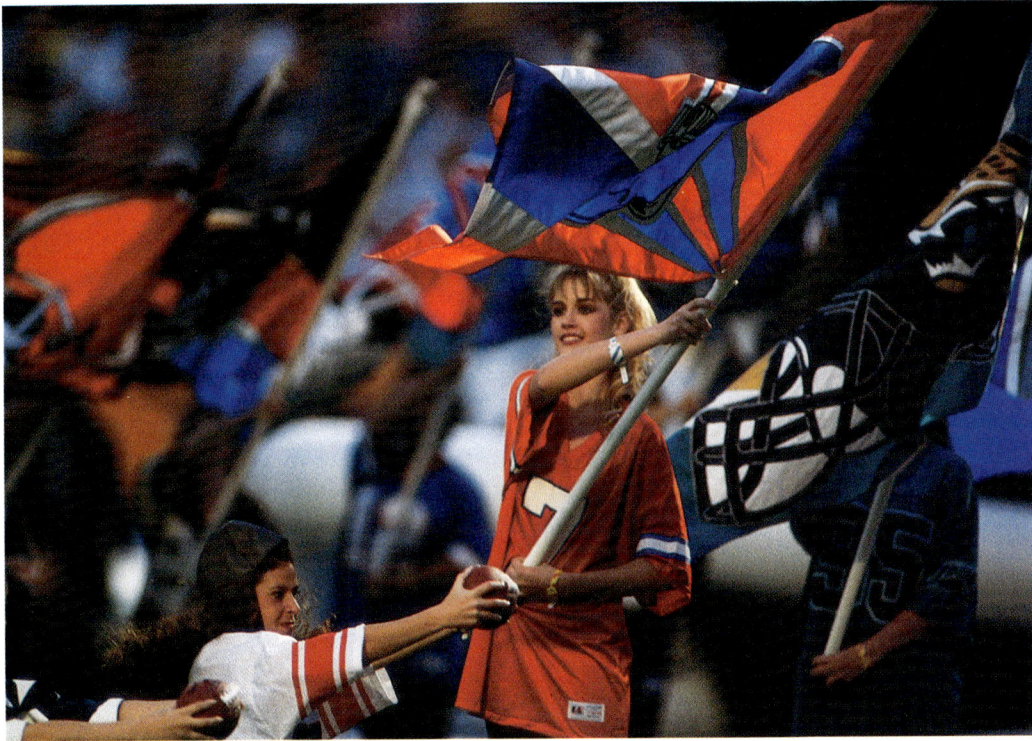

"If I were a Hollywood
screenwriter, this is
how I would have
written the script."
—Gary Plummer

While San Francisco's Deion Sanders (below) and San Diego's Steve Hendrickson (opposite top) stretch, the officials engage in an informal pre-game visit with Commissioner Paul Tagliabue.

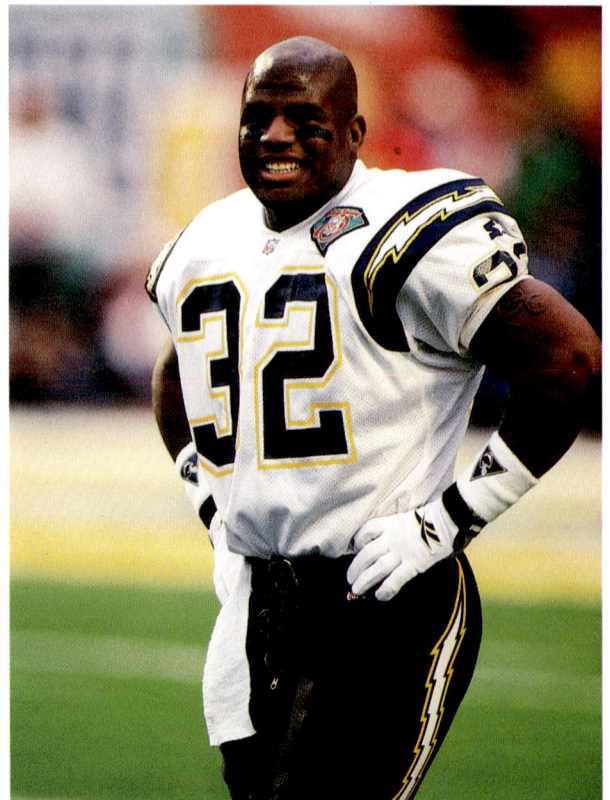

Placekicker Doug Brien and long snapper David Binn (top) were teammates in college but opponents in Super Bowl XXIX. Joe Namath and Don Shula (above) were adversaries in Super Bowl III, one of the most famous Super Bowls ever. Right, Chargers running back Eric Bieniemy. Opposite far right, a pensive 49ers Coach George Seifert.

Everything has to be just right for Jerry Rice and Deion Sanders before they take the field. Sanders' pregame routine includes reviewing Chargers game tapes.

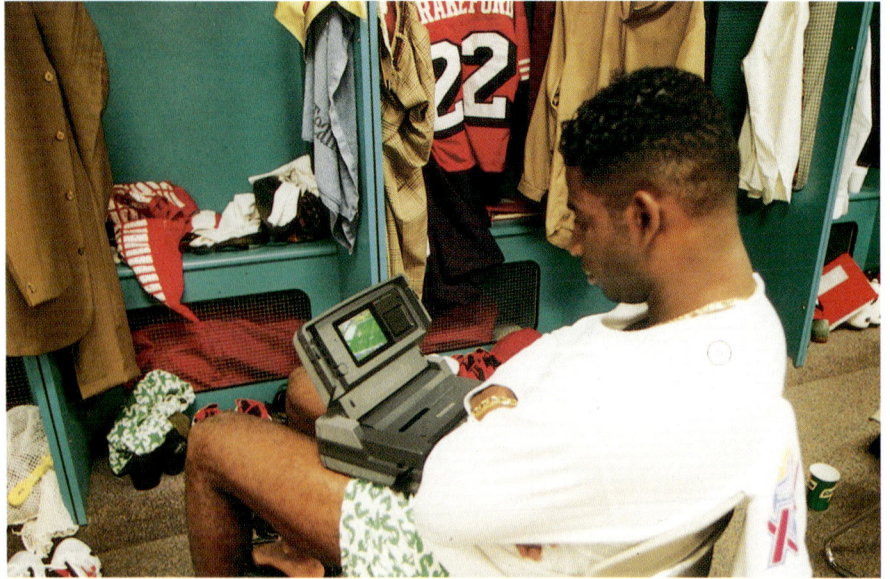

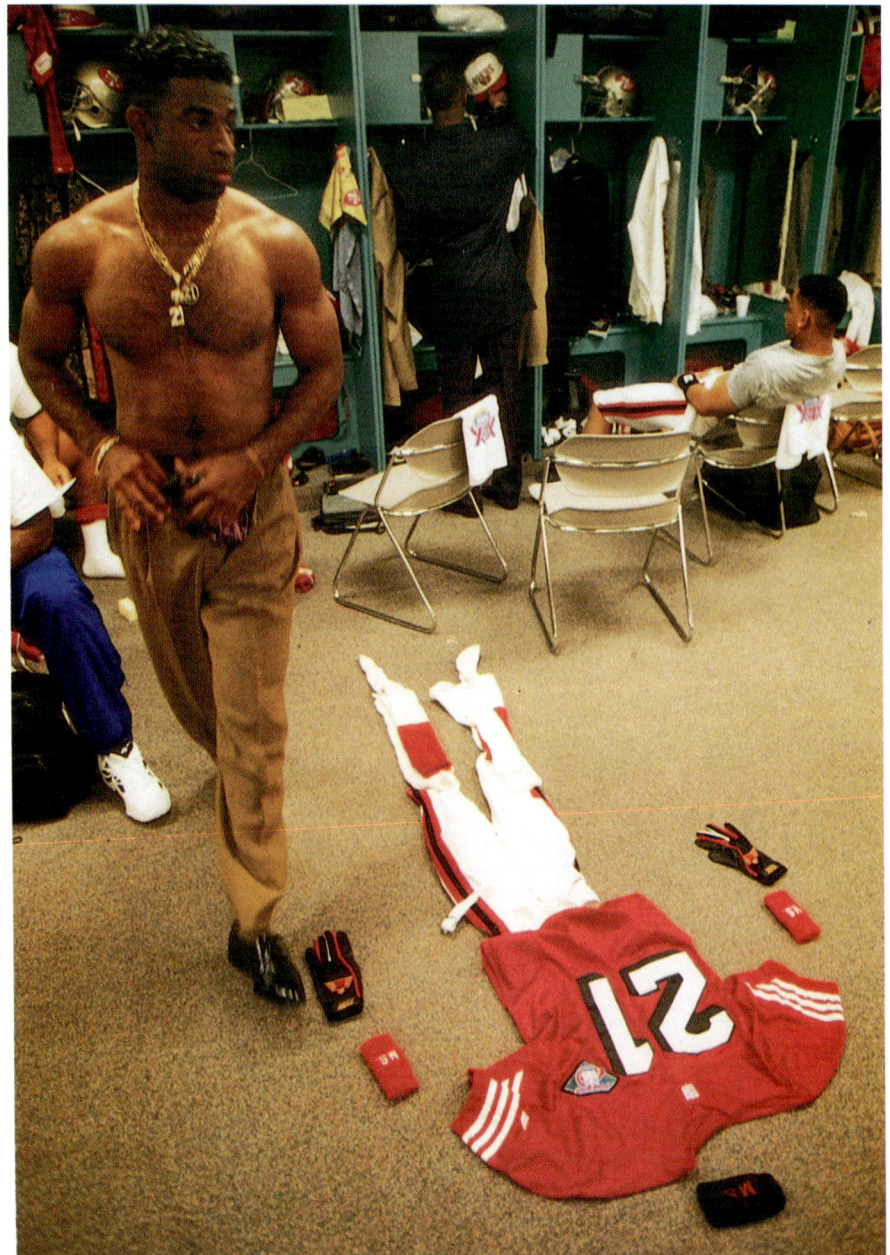

"I'm not an intimidator. I'm a performer. I'm a player. I'm an athlete. I'm an entertainer. I'm all that." —Deion Sanders

"The only thing I try to tell the young guys is to appreciate the moment."   —Jesse Sapolu

Just before game time, George Seifert takes a few moments for himself and Jerry Rice reminds his teammates what they want to accomplish.

"Anything a guy can do in the Super Bowl he'll remember for the rest of his life. If he doesn't do anything, at least he ran through the tunnel."
—Chris Mims

The momentum builds (clockwise from opposite top): Jerry Rice explodes out of the tunnel; the 482nd Fighter Wing performs its precision fly-by; Otto Graham completes the traditional toss of the coin under the watchful eye of Referee Jerry Markbreit, and Kathie Lee Gifford sings "The Star Spangled Banner."

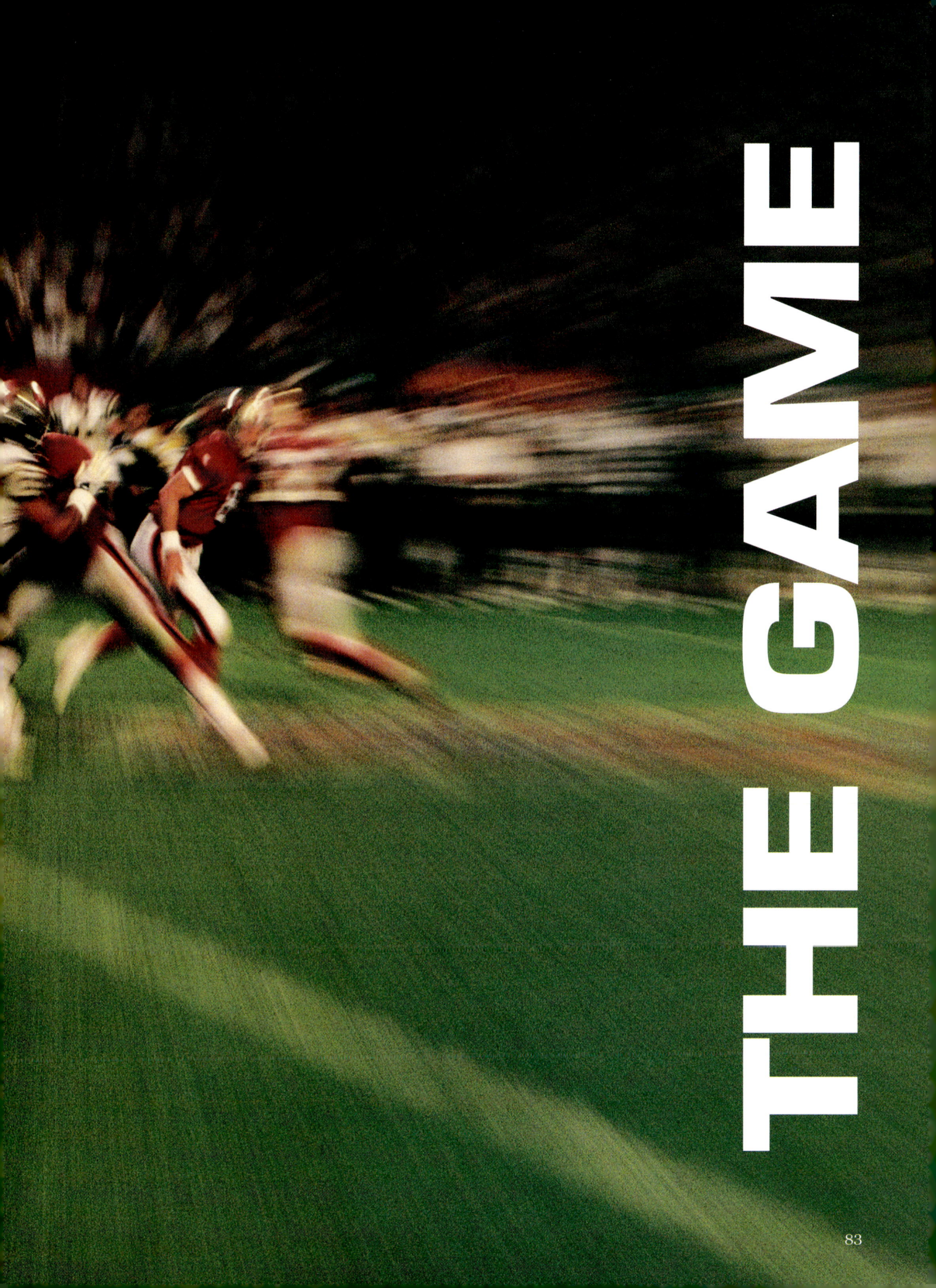

THE GAME

*Finally, game time.
Dexter Carter runs the
kickoff to the 26 and
Steve Young takes over.*

"You'll be able to tell a lot about how the game is going to go by the first quarter. If we go out and get a couple of quick strikes, it puts them in a situation they don't want to be in."
—Bart Oates

Eighty-four seconds into the game, Jerry Rice (opposite) takes a 44-yard pass from Steve Young as the 49ers put the Chargers and Stan Humphries in a hole.

"Steve Young will run into linebackers. He doesn't care."
—Dwayne Harper

"They say the spread is 20 points. Does that mean when we start the game it'll be 49ers 20 and those guys have zero? That doesn't happen."
　　　—Ricky Watters

"The one moment that stands out more than any other in the Super Bowl to me is when Marcus Allen broke that run against the Redskins. That was one of the most beautiful runs I've ever seen. I've always wanted to do something like that, always." —Ricky Watters

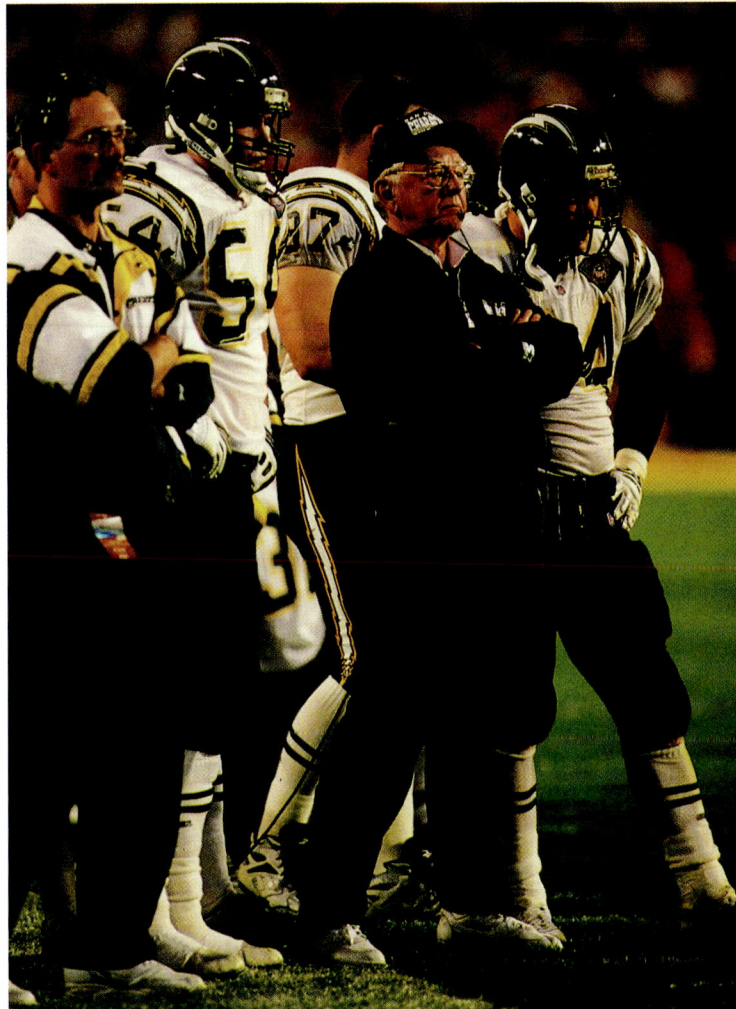

Ricky Watters looks over his shoulder for the ball en route to the end zone (opposite). The 49ers' second touchdown in their first seven plays creates joy for San Francisco but sideline tension for San Diego Defensive Coordinator Bill Arnsparger.

"I told those guys [in December], 'When you get healthy, you're going to wreck somebody.' And now here they are playing us in the Super Bowl."
—Dana Stubblefield

Resilient and unfazed, the Chargers mount a long drive behind the passing of Stan Humphries, the running of Natrone Means and crucial third-down gains by Ronnie Harmon.

Ronnie Harmon outraces Troy Wilson and Natrone Means bursts through a massive hole (opposite) to set up Means' touchdown dive over Bryant Young at the goal line.

"I've been nothing but a running back since I was eight years old. I used to drop my head and run over guys. I used to get unnecessary roughness penalties just for bucking the kids off."

—Natrone Means

Steve Young, John Taylor and Jerry Rice begin another scoring march, halting the Chargers' optimism.

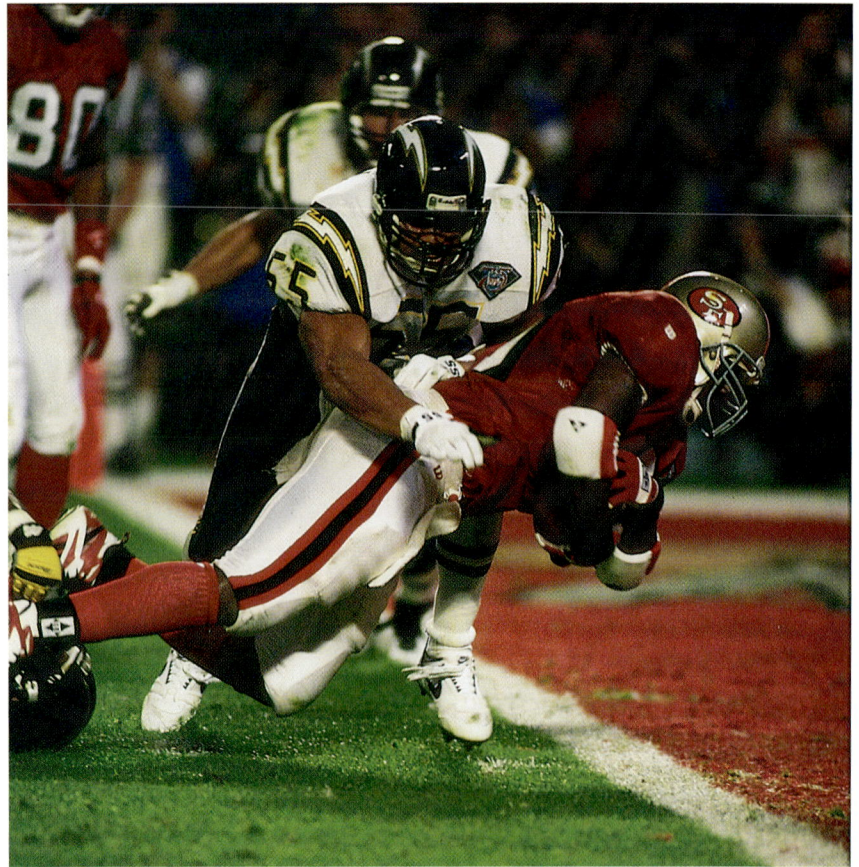

"The fear of
failure motivates
us more than the
motivation of
success."
—Bart Oates

After the 49ers
squeeze out a first
down at the Chargers'
five, William Floyd
takes a short pass
from Steve Young and
struggles past Junior
Seau and David
Griggs for the score.
With the Chargers
trailing 21-7, Natrone
Means tries to break
free; San Diego
defenders huddle
with Coach Bobby
Ross (opposite).

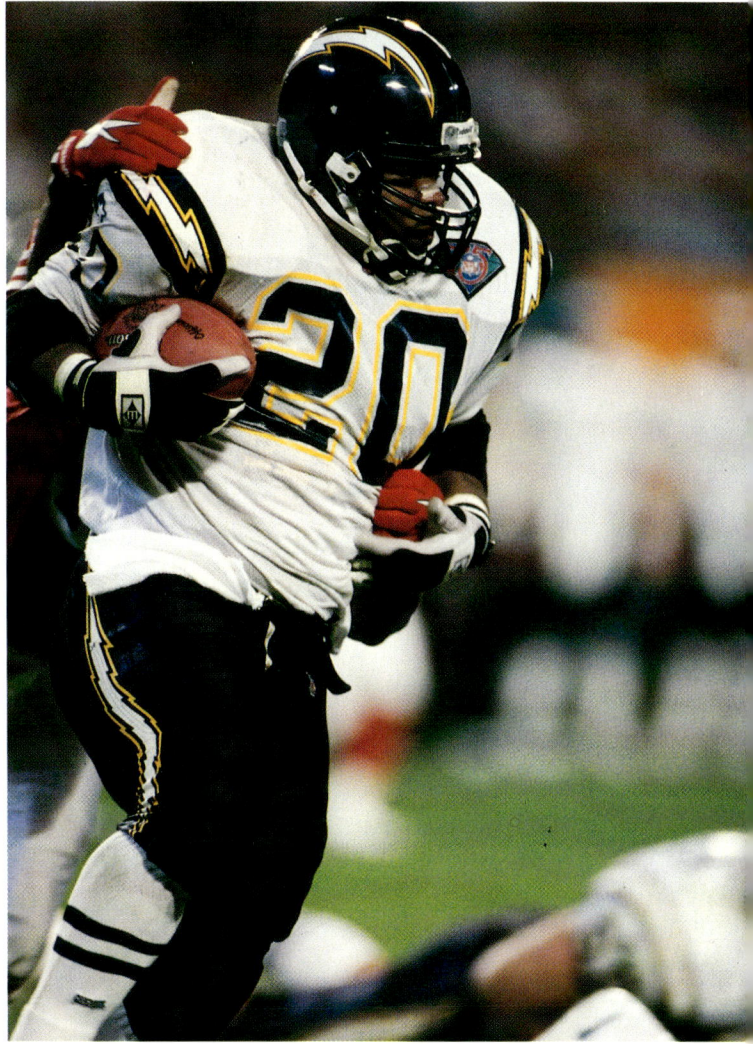

"If something bad happens in the game, he tells us, 'You better not go in the tank. You have to keep fighting.'"
— Tony Martin on Stan Humphries

"I don't believe you can play catch-up against these guys."
—Stan Humphries

The Chargers must punt after Natrone Means finds nothing but 49ers jerseys. Rodney Harrison downs the ball.

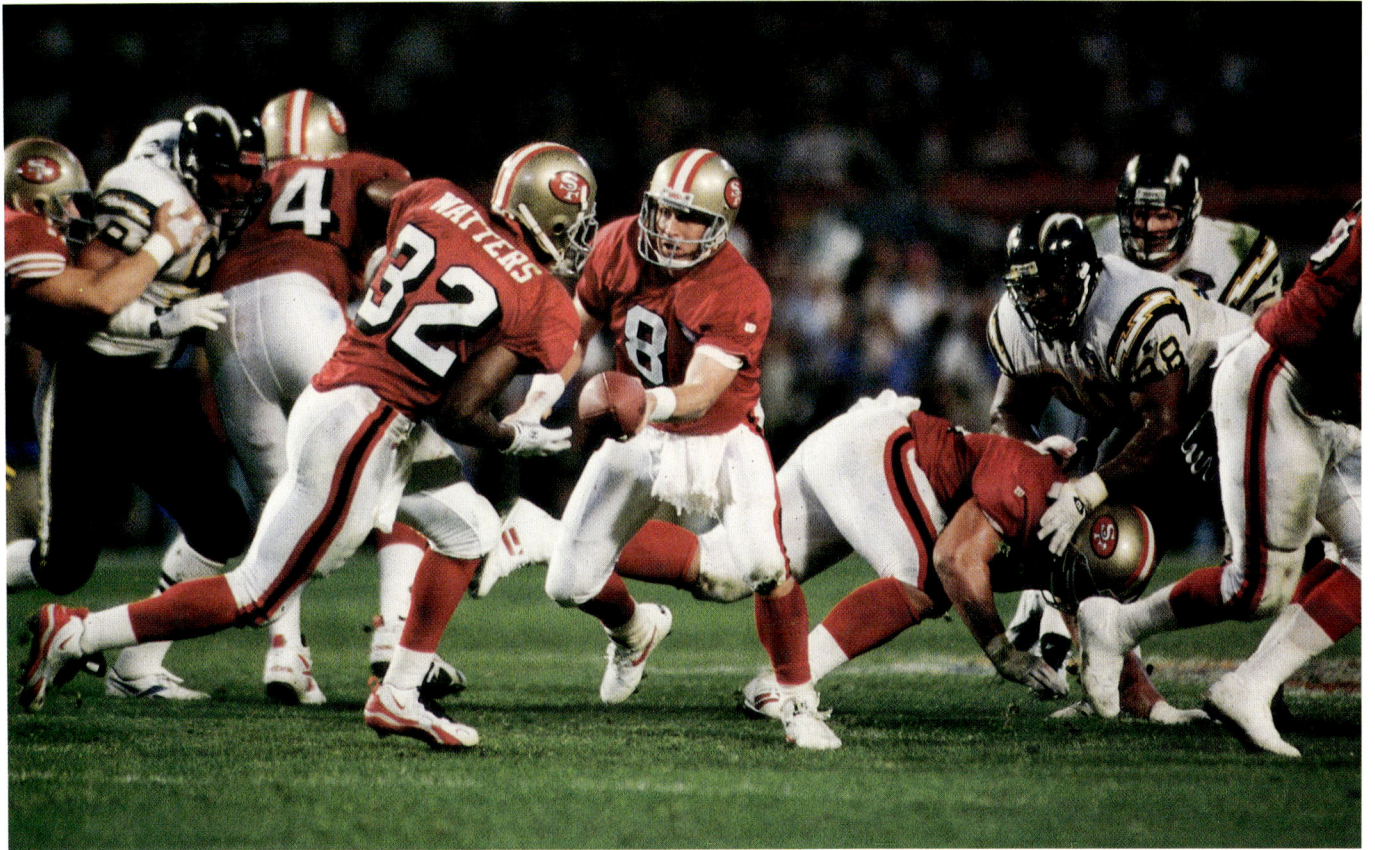

"When Joe Montana ran this offense, it was like he was conducting a symphony. With Steve Young, it's like a jam session. They both produce great music, but it's different."   —Harris Barton

San Francisco, bolstered by Steve Young, Ricky Watters and veteran linemen Jesse Sapolu and Harris Barton, takes the offensive again.

101

Ricky Watters celebrates the 49ers' fourth touchdown of the game – his second of three.

"People say, 'Is there any chance for a letdown?' This is the Super Bowl! Letdown! What are you letting down for?"
　　　　　—Ricky Watters

Eric Bieniemy provides some cheer with a big gain on a pass from Stan Humphries, leading up to a field goal by John Carney close to the end of the half. But Deion Sanders and the rest of the 49ers continue to shadow San Diego.

With extravagant costumes and effects, halftime at the Super Bowl harkens back to ancient rituals combining sport with entertainment.

Halftime fireworks create a mystical midfield scene where Deion Sanders and Merton Hanks convene right before the start of the third quarter. Opposite, Doug Brien kicks off.

A Stan Humphries
pass is dropped on
third down, but the
Chargers' defense gets
a promising second-
half start: Rodney
Harrison stops punt
returner Dexter Carter
(opposite top) and
Raylee Johnson (99)
and Leslie O'Neal (91)
sack Steve Young
(below). Still, the
49ers continue to score
as Ricky Watters cele-
brates his third TD.

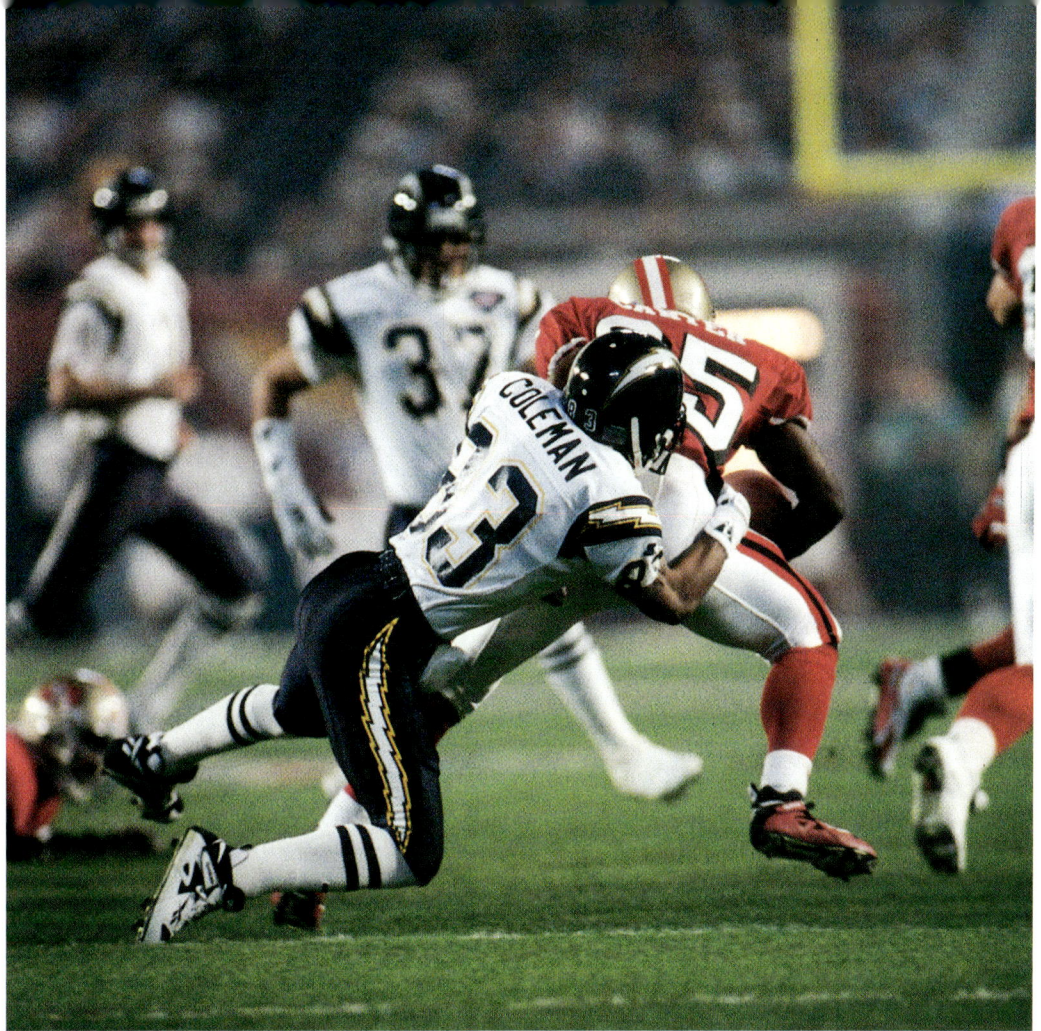

"We are playing the
AFC Champion.
There is no such
thing as us being
overconfident."
    —Merton Hanks

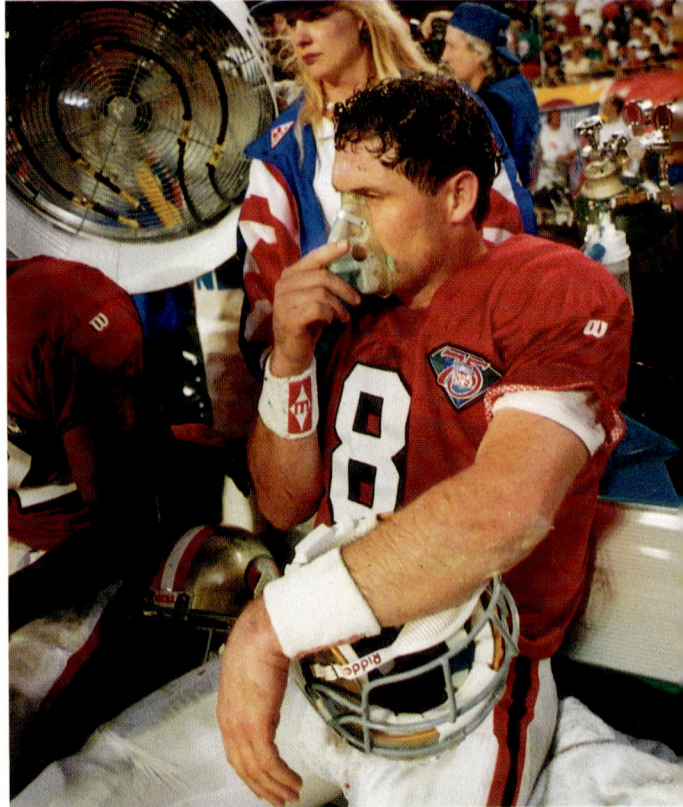

"To see Rickey Jackson and Gary Plummer enjoy this after being in the league so long gives me the satisfaction I've gotten this year."
—Jesse Sapolu

With Leslie O'Neal in pursuit (opposite), Steve Young rolls left, then takes a breather. Steve Wallace squares himself to protect his quarterback. Left, former Saints teammates Rickey Jackson and Stan Brock go head-to-head; below, ex-Chargers teammates Gary Plummer and Steve Hendrickson.

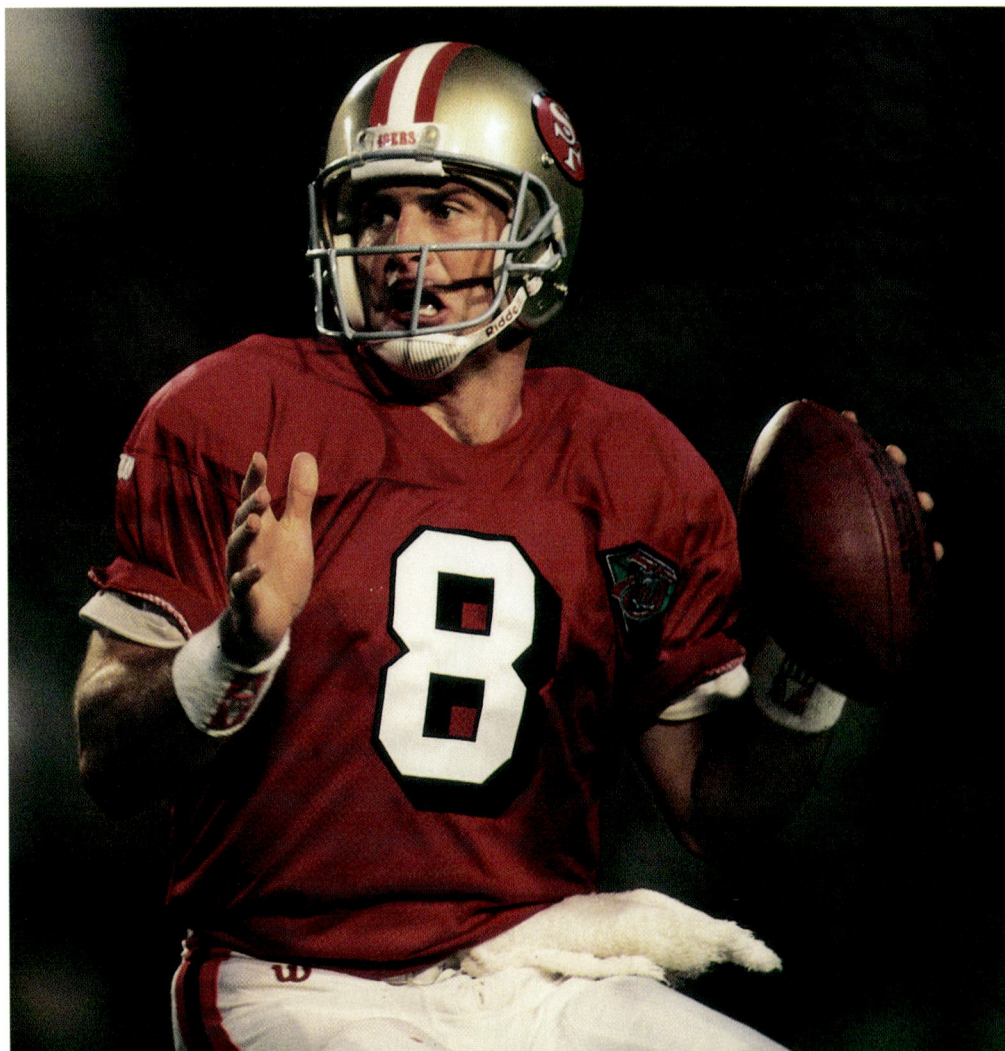

Steve Young and Jerry Rice connect for San Francisco's sixth touchdown, but the Chargers come right back with Andre Coleman's 98-yard kickoff return (opposite).

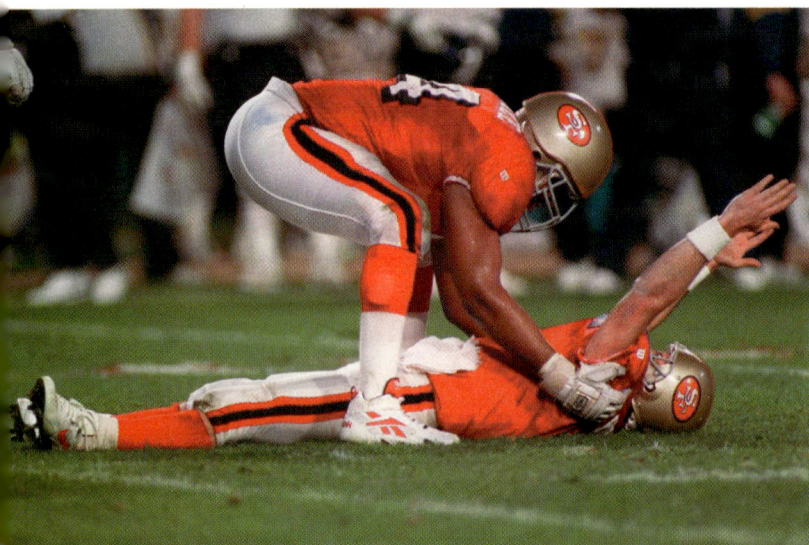

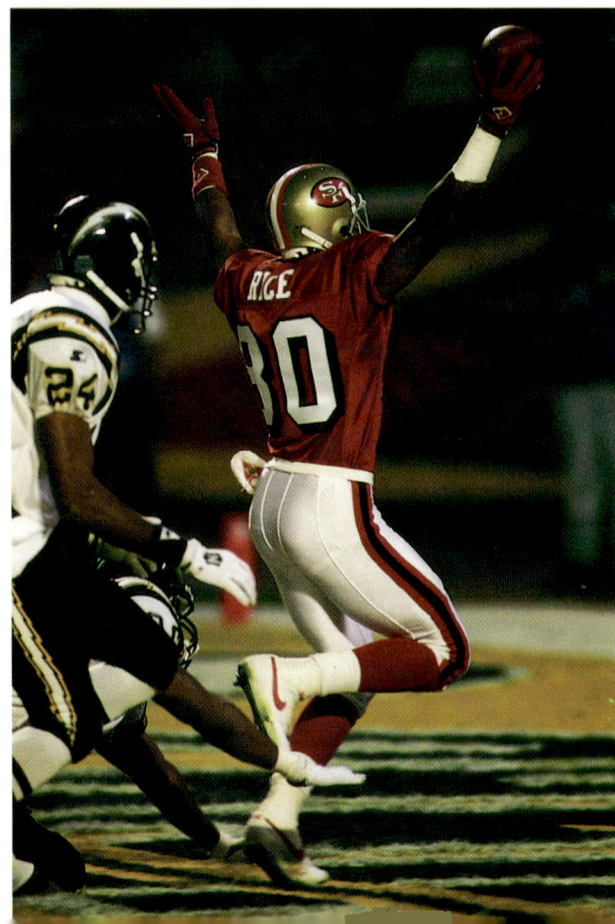

"People were talking about our winning streak four, five, six, seven games into it. I said, 'This is no streak, man, this is what we do.'"
—Steve Young

Mark Seay (82), Alfred Pupunu (86) and Isaac Davis celebrate a two-point conversion. Opposite, Natrone Means searches desperately, and ultimately in vain, for running room on fourth down.

"Jerry, as you
know, is pos-
sessed to get to
the end zone."
—Steve Young

Chris Mims deflects a Steve Young pass (opposite), but the 49ers soon score again when Rice tumbles into the end zone where he momentarily sits (left).

119

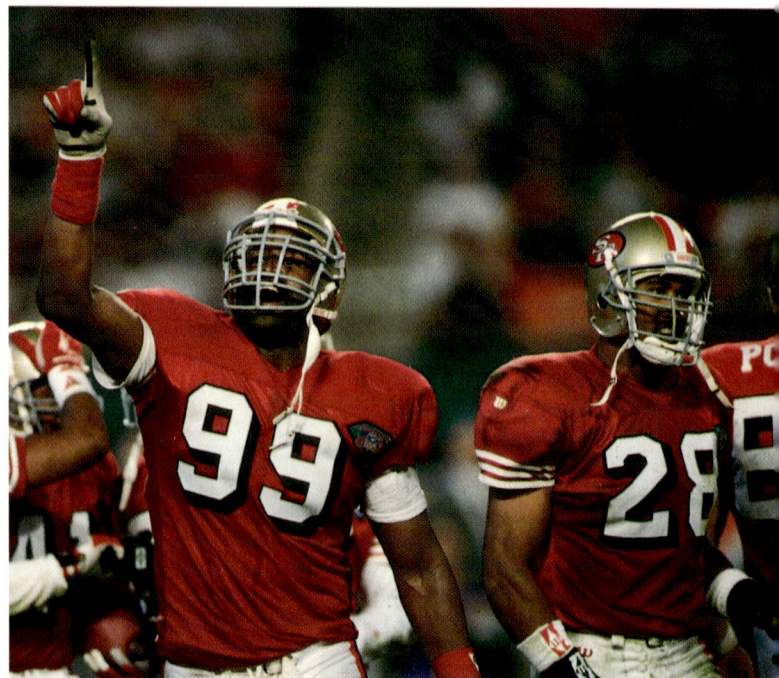

Clockwise from top, Ed McCaffrey stops Andre Coleman's return and Stan Humphries' injury necessitates bringing in Gale Gilbert, who scrambles eight yards before Dennis Brown's tackle. Victory nears for the 49ers: Tim Harris celebrates and Jerry Rice and Steve Young embrace in tired relief.

"Ronnie Lott told me in my rookie year, 'Until you get one of these rings, you're just another guy that played the game.'"
—Eric Davis

Opposite, Deion Sanders and Toi Cook halt San Diego's fading hopes with interceptions. Mark Seay (left) runs free and Tony Martin (bottom) chases down a Stan Humphries pass, but Bobby Ross knows time is running out.

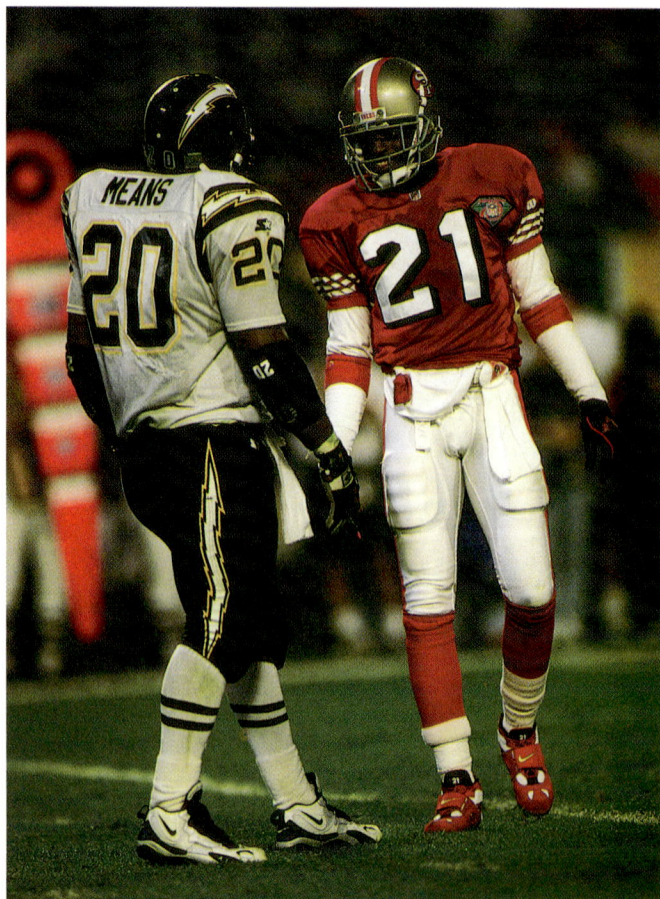

A variety of emotions surface as players accept the outcome. Clockwise from top left, Raylee Johnson; Toi Cook and Tim McDonald; Deion Sanders with Natrone Means; and Dana Stubblefield and a teammate.
Opposite, Steve Young.

PORTRAIT OF A CHAMPION

By Ronnie Lott

The game of football has been compared most often to war. The analogy is appropriate because of the methods the coaches (generals) use to design their offensive and defensive strategies and the way the players (soldiers) prepare their minds and bodies for the game (battle). But that comparison is limiting because it ignores an important aspect – that football is a game, and it is a game of beauty. That aspect has kept me in the game for 14 seasons and will keep me, if I am fortunate, for one more. A single football game can be a work of art, and in Super Bowl XXIX the San Francisco 49ers painted a masterpiece.

With every stroke from the first to the last, the 49ers worked with precision, clarity, confidence and purpose. They knew exactly what they wanted to create. There was no initial experimental stroke to get the feel of the brush or the texture of the canvas. They were out to paint the greatest work of art they were capable of, which is a direct product of the greatness the players, coaches and franchise had experienced before. That's why they were successful so early in the game, scoring three touchdowns on their first three possessions on the way to a 49-26 victory. They knew going into the game that it was in their best interests to get ahead at the beginning because they were facing a ball-control team, and a ball-control team like the Chargers can't be in the position to control the ball if it is behind.

Simply put, the San Francisco 49ers were out to achieve greatness, which is the mentality a team must have going into a game with as great a magnitude as the Super Bowl. It is the same mentality required of artists who desire to perfect their craft.

Staying with that analogy, the San Diego Chargers performed as if they were first-year art students. They had great talent and promise, and they were working with the best kinds of tools. But they were tentative in their approach, as if it were their first time sitting down at the stool, their first time holding the brush, their first time touching the canvas. To paint a great picture or to win a great game, you must have a championship mentality: make the great strokes, make the championship plays. The 49ers had it, the Chargers didn't.

A lot of people asked me if I had mixed feelings about Super Bowl XXIX. I was a member of the 49ers for 10 seasons and won four Super Bowls with them. The greatest years of my career were with the 49ers and some of my greatest memories are of my days in the Bay Area. I still live there. But I've been away from the team for four seasons. In 1991 and 1992 I was trying to help get the Los Angeles Raiders to the Super Bowl and in 1993 and 1994 I was trying to help the New York Jets get there.

I wasn't happy to leave the 49ers, but I refuse to have bitterness about it or jealousy towards my former teammates who were fortunate enough to play in Super Bowl XXIX. Before I played in my last Super Bowl – XXIV, when we defeated Denver in the Louisiana Superdome – I had a long talk with Jack Lambert, who had been in and won four Super Bowls with the Pittsburgh Steelers. He said, unless he was playing, that it never mattered to him which teams were in the Super Bowl. What mattered were the people. He said he admired and envied the people who were playing in it because he knew how special it was to be in that spotlight. That attitude epitomizes the mark of a true champion, and that's how I have always tried to carry myself. So my only thoughts about Super Bowl XXIX were those of excitement for the players – especially the older veterans – who had never been there before. Of course, there were times when I couldn't help but feel that I could have been there or try to figure out the reasons why I wasn't there, but it all boils down to the same thing: the players and teams who get there have done all the things they were supposed to do, and for that the 49ers and Chargers deserve total admiration and credit.

Playing in the Super Bowl is a special moment and practically every player who has played in one will cherish the memory forever. Winning one is truly the ultimate experience. In many ways, it can be compared to getting married or experiencing the birth of your child. That's not an overblown comparison, certainly not one for a competitive athlete. Your marriage may end, your children will move away, your relationships will change. But you'll always have special moments of shared experience. Your greatest moments in life always involve other people.

Once you've played in a Super Bowl, you can't help but want to go back again. Even if you never come close to making the Hall of Fame, you still will be recognized as one of the best players at that time if you play in a Super Bowl. Is there really any other pure motivation? Ask that question of Deion Sanders, who came to the 49ers in 1994 for much less money than he could have gotten elsewhere, strictly because he knew that playing in San Francisco was his best chance to get to the Super Bowl. People know Deion as "Prime Time," but most of all Deion wants to be known as a winner.

The Super Bowl is immense. The magnitude of it cannot be described adequately. The distractions are everywhere. When we were fighting the Gulf War in 1991, a good deal of the coverage of the Super Bowl involved how our troops would be able to watch the game. Imagine that! We're fighting to preserve democracy in the world and we're worried that our soldiers won't be able to watch the Super Bowl! That's big. People who never watch a sporting event the entire year stop to watch the Super Bowl. Entire convents of nuns watch the Super Bowl. Media members who don't know the difference between a tackle and a block come to interview players they've never heard of. It's true that I played in front of bigger crowds several times for USC, but hundreds of millions of people around the world watch the Super Bowl on television in addition to the 75,000 or so who see it in person. When you take those things into account and realize the players have to perform on a stage of such grand scale – players who are painfully aware that any minor mistake they make will be blown into huge proportions – it's impossible not to have an appreciation for the greatness they are able to exhibit in the face of such pressure.

Obviously, the 49ers have built up a tolerance for that pressure. In fact, when they don't have that pressure, they don't perform as well. An interesting thing about the 49ers of 1994 is that they brought in so many new faces. But the great majority of the new players knew exactly what it took to deal with that pressure because they had so much experience playing against the 49ers in the past. Rickey Jackson and Toi Cook played against the 49ers twice every season for the New Orleans Saints. Deion Sanders and Tim McDonald were no strangers to the 49ers' way. As a member of the Chargers, Gary Plummer played against the 49ers at least once a year in the preseason. In that respect, these players actually had that championship mentality even though they had never played in the Super Bowl before. And, of course, Ken Norton with Dallas, Bart Oates with the Giants, Charles Mann with the Redskins and Richard Dent with the Chicago Bears – all 49ers in 1994 – had already succeeded on that Super Bowl stage.

That is where the Chargers faced their greatest disadvantage. It is true that they didn't match up well with San Francisco in terms of personnel because the 49ers had great players and depth at every position, whereas the Chargers had holes in several areas, specifically in the defensive secondary. But football history is full of instances in which weaker teams have won. In Super Bowl XXIX, the Chargers definitely had a good scheme, they were well-prepared and their players were courageous; they kept playing hard and kept trying to score, which isn't always apparent in championship games. The image of an injured Stan Humphries fighting to return to the game in the fourth quarter continues to be a lasting impression.

The Chargers' main weakness was their lack of a championship attitude. They didn't know – and probably couldn't have known – what it takes. On practically every drive, there was at least one play in a crucial situation where they didn't come through the way a champion needs to come through. Dropped passes, penalties, missed blocks or tackles . . . the list is long.

But now they know. With that experience, combined with the leadership and personnel expertise of Bobby Beathard and Bobby Ross, their youth in key areas and their ownership's desire to bring in the right free agents, a case can be made that San Diego will be an AFC force through the turn of the century.

Still, there's one more barrier facing the Chargers and every other AFC team: the NFC is a vastly superior conference and will continue to be for the foreseeable future unless a major institutional change is made.

Some Super Bowl-winning teams alter the face of the NFL. The Jets did it in III, San Francisco did it in XVI, the Bears and Giants did it in XX and XXI. The 49ers' win in XXIX won't affect how other teams do their business – that's already happening – but San Francisco's dominance could have an indirect impact.

But that's only if the NFL undergoes the very difficult and traumatic transformation of realigning its conferences.

Conference strength does go in cycles; in fact, when the 49ers began their rise the AFC was still the dominant conference, having won 11 of 13 NFL championships between 1969 and 1981. But franchises have moved or are moving from one city to another, the league is expanding and the nature of the game is changing faster than ever. Some long-time rivalries have eroded, but realignment can create even stronger rivalries, which can only help the league.

The NFC has now reigned in the Super Bowl for 11 straight years. The reason for its dominance is the same as the AFC's previous dominance: it plays a more physical style of football. It's Darwinism; survival of the fittest. Teams within the conferences struggle to stay with the pack, and so they must improve or fall by the wayside. There are more good teams in the NFC. As a result, there are more pressure games in that conference later in the season, and therefore the NFC team is better prepared for the pressure of the Super Bowl. You can't say that about the AFC. I played in some big games for the Jets last season, particularly against Miami, and the magnitude was just not the same.

San Diego wasn't prepared in that regard, certainly not as well as the 49ers were. Some AFC teams are moving in the right direction, such as New England, Pittsburgh and Cleveland – all of them are assuming the attitude and nature of an NFC team – but as we look to the 1995 season, the concentration of strength remains in the NFC. Specifically, it resides in San Francisco, where fans are enjoying the first true sports dynasty in several years. The 49ers have now won five Super Bowls, more than any other team in NFL history. Even more impressive is that they've won at least 10 games in the regular season for 12 straight years. That statistic guarantees their status as a dynasty, and that dynasty is in no threat of dying.

The 49ers have exhibited over and over the ability to maintain high quality. They've never had to rebuild; rather, they retool when and where necessary. Everybody in the organization – from the owner to the young receptionists – takes pride in being the best. When a key person leaves, whether it's a player or a coach such as Offensive Coordinator Mike Shanahan (to become head coach of the Denver Broncos) or Defensive Coordinator Ray Rhodes (to become head coach of the Philadelphia Eagles), the 49ers locate, without panic, the right man to replace the one they've lost. The core, in terms of tradition and style, will remain constant. Eddie DeBartolo and Carmen Policy see to that. So much has been made about Shanahan's brilliant play-calling – which it was – but few remember that fans were extremely worried when Shanahan's predecessor, Mike Holmgren, left to become head coach of the Green Bay Packers.

The point is, transition is a necessary part of sport; the landscape always changes.

It just means there's another opportunity for other people to paint their own masterpiece.

AFTERMATH

131

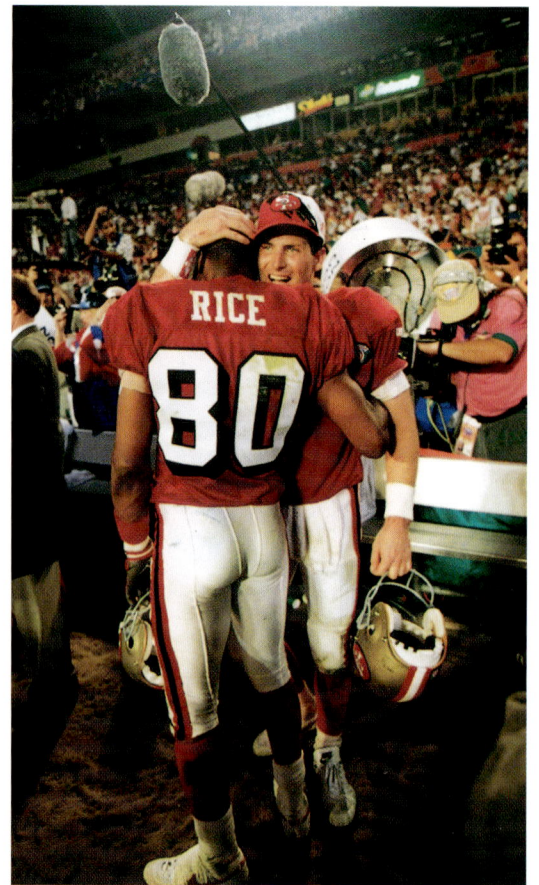

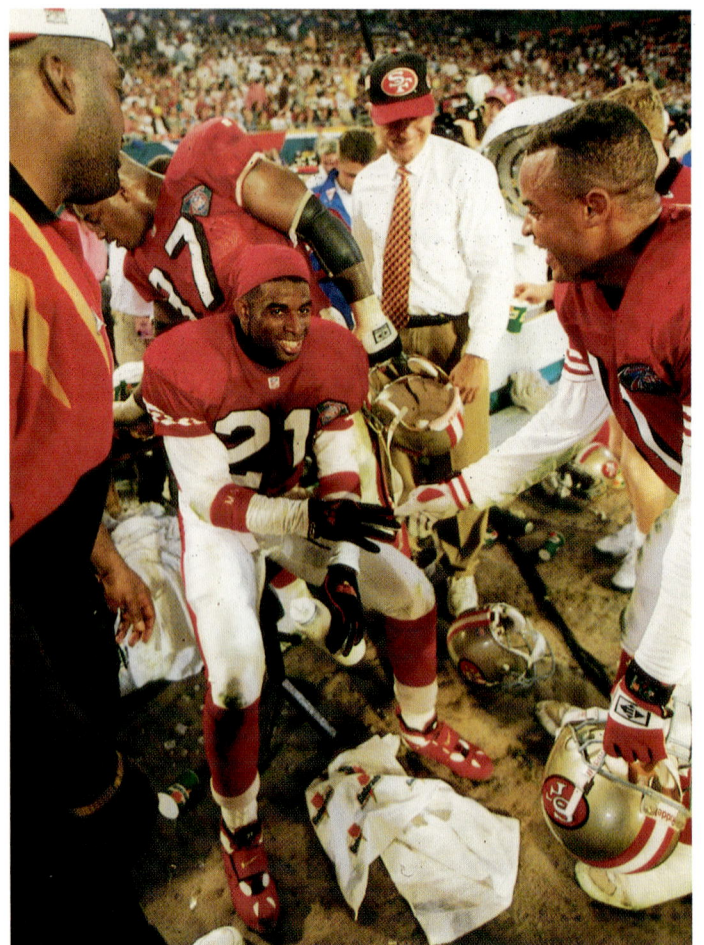

Clockwise from top left: Eddie DeBartolo Jr., celebrates with Rickey Jackson; Steve Young and Jerry Rice embrace; Sanders and Toi Cook; quarterbacks coach Gary Kubiak with Young. Opposite, Gary Plummer with sons Grant and Garrett; Young; Ken Norton Jr., and Junior Seau; Rice.

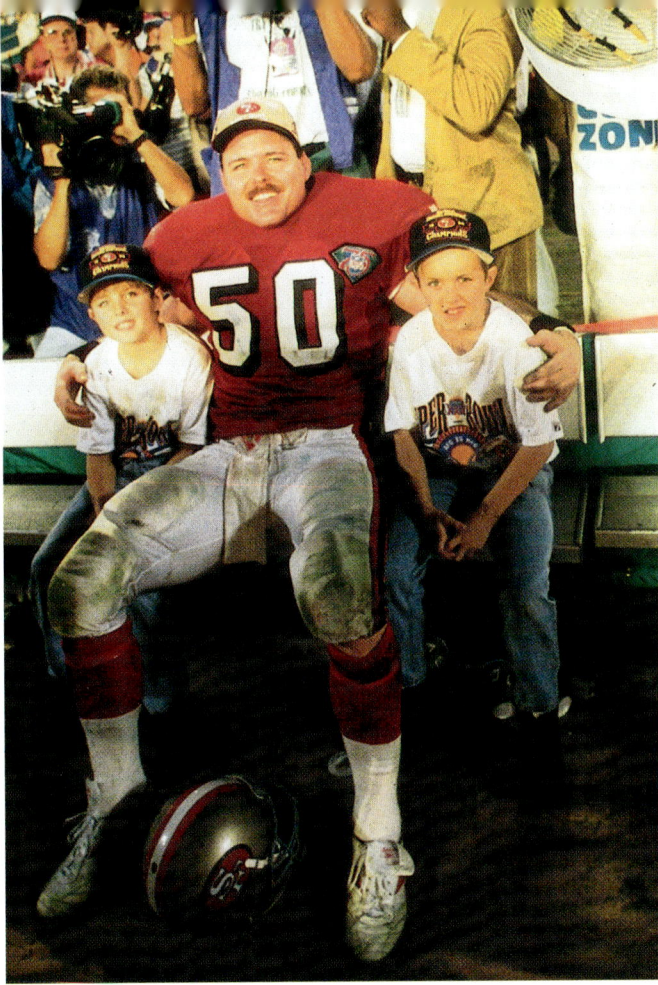

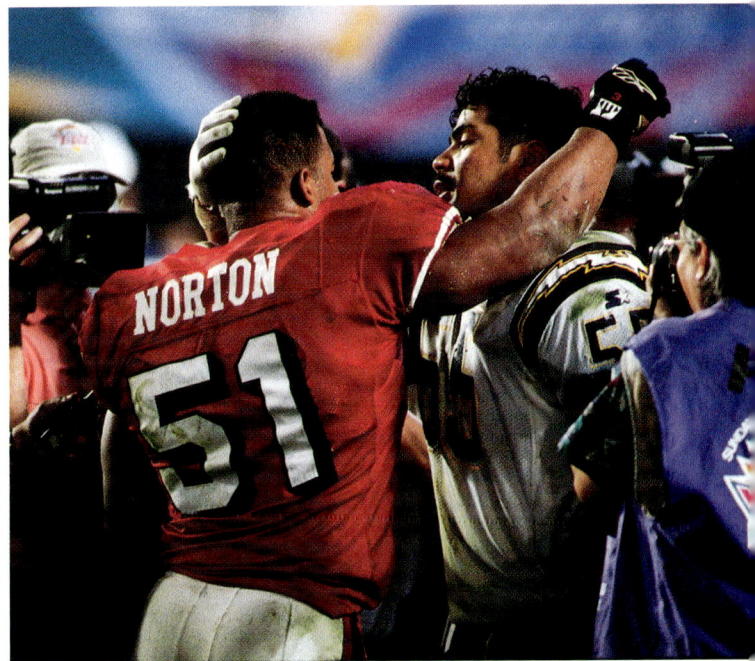

"That's maybe some of the best football that's ever been played."   —Steve Young

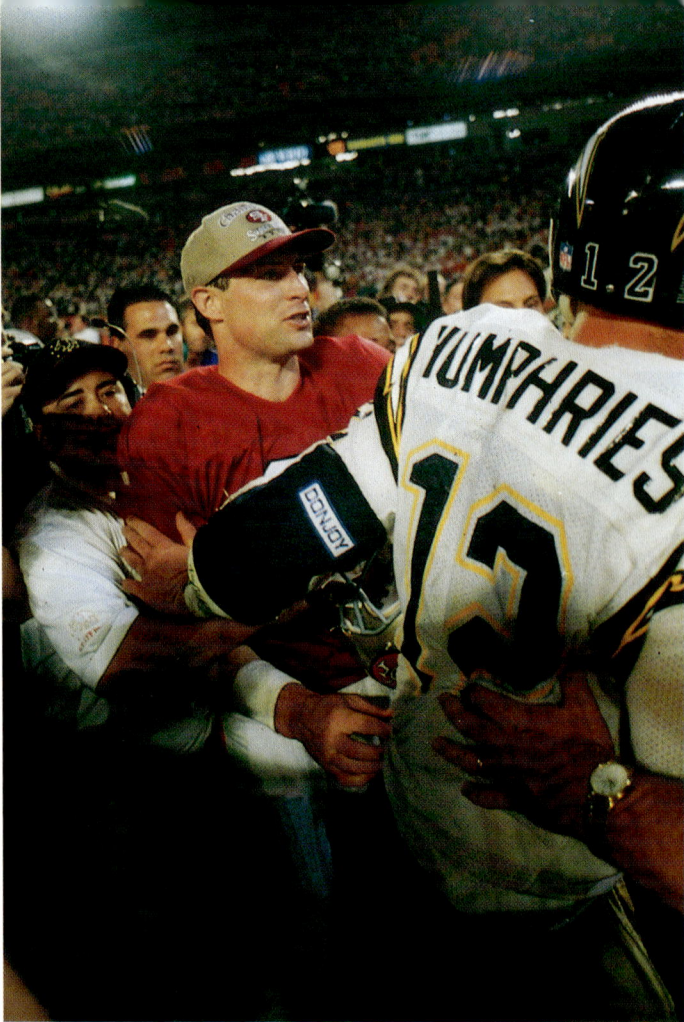

Clockwise from left: The quarterbacks; Rickey Jackson and son; George Seifert gets drenched; Steve Young and Eddie DeBartolo Jr. Opposite, Young and Jerry Rice celebrate; DeBartolo and 49ers President Carmen Policy; DeBartolo, Policy and Seifert; DeBartolo talks with President Clinton; Junior Seau.

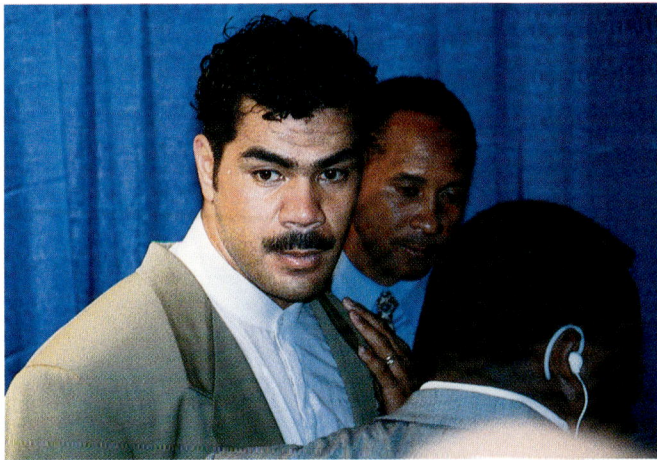

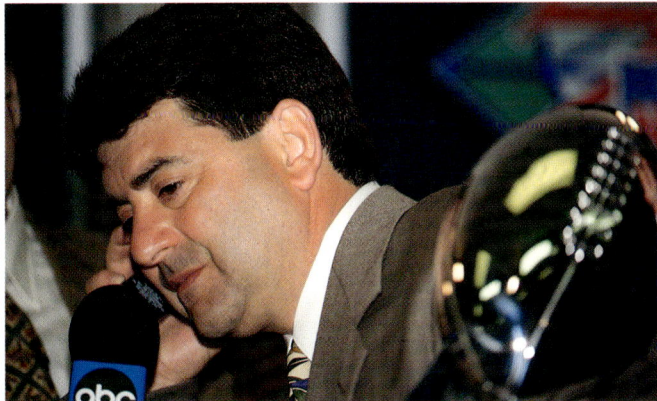

Steve Young clutches his big prize as George Seifert, Deion Sanders and Bobby Ross offer their insights. Meanwhile, the cleanup begins almost immediately on the stadium grounds.

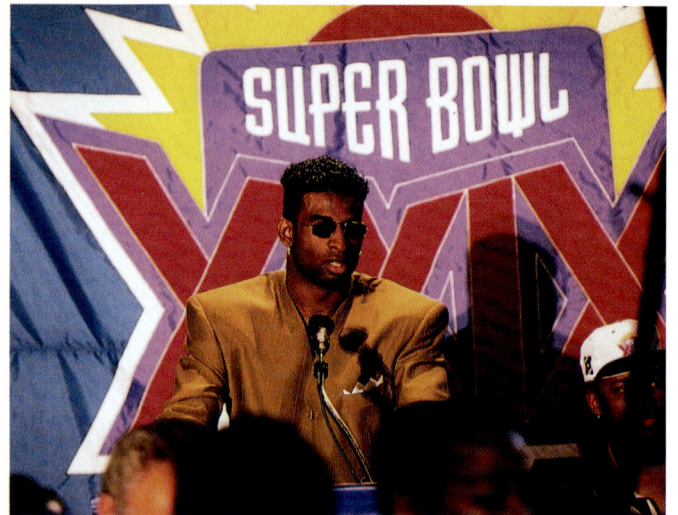

The Chargers, still champions in their fans' hearts, return to a heartfelt parade through San Diego. Opposite, middle right, Owner Alex Spanos and General Manager Bobby Beathard begin plotting their strategy for next season.

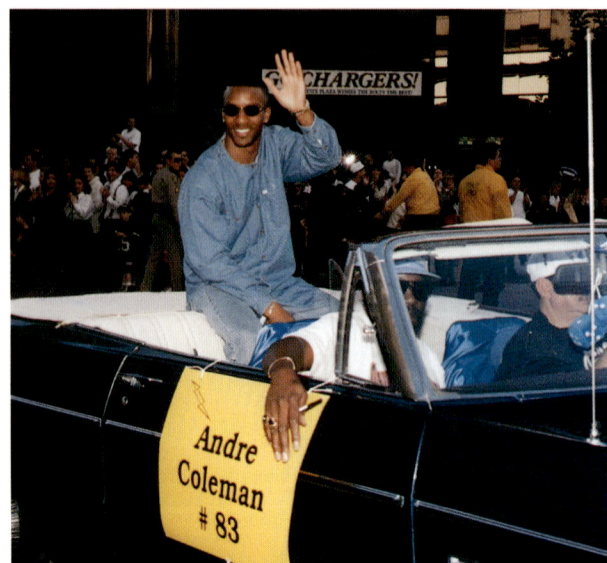

Joe Cocozzo #69

Dennis Gibson

Andre Coleman #83

"The Bolt will be back."
—Reuben Davis

Next pages: The 49ers' celebration begins for their fans in San Francisco as soon as the game ends, then culminates with a huge Monday parade down Market Street.

David Griggs #92

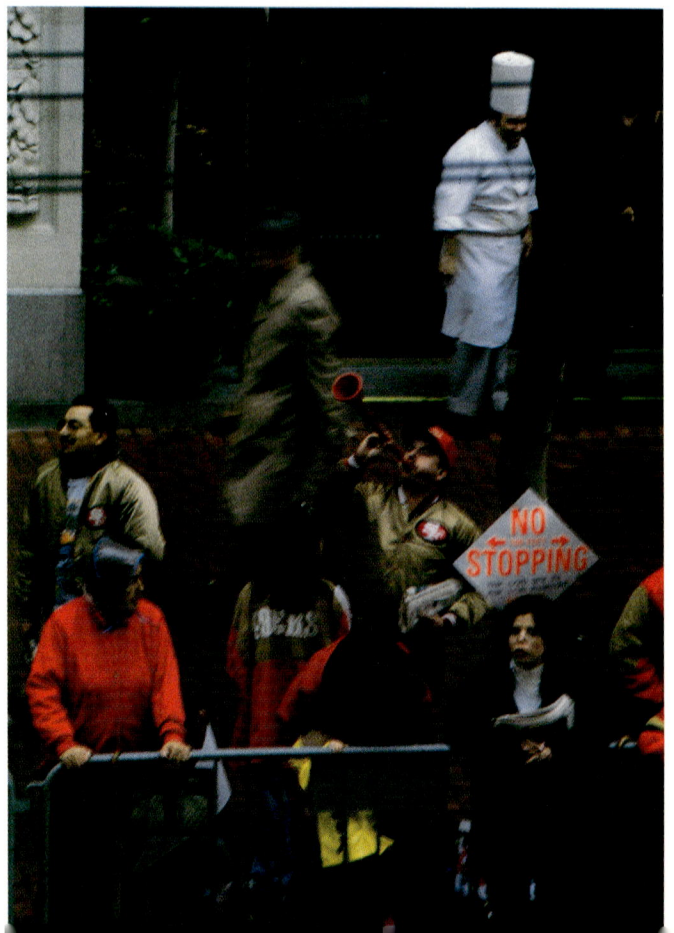

An estimated crowd of 300,000 lines Market Street to show their appreciation, and the 49ers respond in kind. Top left, Jesse Sapolu; middle left, Dana Stubblefield and Bryant Young; bottom, line coach Bobb McKittrick and his wife, Teckla.

APPENDIX

SUPER BOWL XXIX
Joe Robbie Stadium, Miami
January 29, 1995

San Diego Chargers	7	3	8	8—26
San Francisco 49ers	14	14	14	7—49

Attendance: 74,107. Time of game: 3:36.

SCORING PLAYS

49ers, First Quarter, 13:36: Jerry Rice scores on a 44-yard pass play from Steve Young. Doug Brien kicks the extra point. Scoring drive: 59 yards, 3 plays, 1:24.

49ers, First Quarter, 10:05: Ricky Watters scores on a 51-yard pass play from Steve Young. Doug Brien kicks the extra point. Scoring drive: 79 yards, 4 plays, 1:53.

Chargers, First Quarter, 2:44: Natrone Means scores on a 1-yard run. John Carney kicks the extra point. Scoring drive: 78 yards, 13 plays, 7:21.

49ers, Second Quarter, 13:02: William Floyd scores on a 5-yard pass play from Steve Young. Doug Brien kicks the extra point. Scoring drive: 70 yards, 10 plays, 4:42.

49ers, Second Quarter, 4:44: Ricky Watters scores on an 8-yard pass play from Steve Young. Doug Brien kicks the extra point. Scoring drive: 49 yards on 9 plays, 4:51.

Chargers, Second Quarter, 1:44: John Carney kicks a 31-yard field goal. Scoring drive: 62 yards, 8 plays, 3:00.

49ers, Third Quarter, 9:35: Ricky Watters scores on a 9-yard run. Doug Brien kicks the extra point. Scoring drive: 62 yards, 7 plays, 3:45.

49ers, Third Quarter, 3:18: Jerry Rice scores on a 15-yard pass play from Steve Young. Doug Brien kicks the extra point. Scoring drive: 67 yards, 10 plays, 4:07.

Chargers, Third Quarter, 3:01: Andre Coleman scores on a 98-yard kickoff return. Mark Seay scores the 2-point conversion on a pass from Stan Humphries.

49ers, Fourth Quarter, 13:49: Jerry Rice scores on a 7-yard pass play from Steve Young. Doug Brien kicks the extra point. Scoring drive: 32 yards, 6 plays, 1:19.

Chargers, Fourth Quarter, 2:25: Tony Martin scores on a 30-yard pass from Stan Humphries. Scoring drive: 32 yards, 6 plays, 1:19. Alfred Pupunu scores the 2-point conversion on a pass from Stan Humphries. Scoring drive: 67 yards, 8 plays, 1:56.

STARTING LINEUPS

San Diego Chargers

Offense			Defense		
No.	Player	Position	No.	Player	Position
80	Shawn Jefferson	wide receiver	94	Chris Mims	defensive end
72	Harry Swayne	left tackle	98	Shawn Lee	defensive tackle
73	Isaac Davis	left guard	93	Reuben Davis	defensive tackle
53	Courtney Hall	center	91	Leslie O'Neal	defensive end
68	Joe Cocozzo	right guard	92	David Griggs	outside linebacker
67	Stan Brock	right tackle	57	Dennis Gibson	inside linebacker
87	Duane Young	tight end	55	Junior Seau	inside linebacker
82	Mark Seay	wide receiver	21	Darrien Gorden	cornerback
12	Stan Humphries	quarterback	28	Dwayne Harper	cornerback
86	Alfred Pupunu	tight end	29	Darren Carrington	strong safety
20	Natrone Means	running back	24	Stanley Richard	free safety

Others

3 John Carney, kicker; 9 Bryan Wagner, punter; 13 Gale Gilbert, quarterback; 25 Sean Vanhorse, cornerback; 31 Willie Clark, running back; 32 Eric Bieniemy, running back; 33 Ronnie Harmon, running back; 34 Steve Hendrickson, tight end-linebacker; 35 Rodney Culver, running back; 37 Rodney Harrison, safety; 44 Eric Castle, tight end; 50 David Binn, long snapper; 54 Doug Miller, linebacker; 58 Lewis Bush, tackle; 64 Curtis Whitley, center-guard; 70 Vaughn Parker, tackle; 74 Eric Jonassen, wide receiver; 81 Tony Martin, wide receiver; 83 Andre Coleman, tight end; 89 Shannon Mitchell, defensive tackle; 95 Les Miller, defensive tackle; 97 John Parrella, defensive tackle; 99 Raylee Johnson, defensive end.

San Francisco 49ers

Offense			Defense		
No.	Player	Position	No.	Player	Position
82	John Taylor	wide receiver	96	Dennis Brown	defensive end
74	Steve Wallace	left tackle	97	Bryant Young	defensive tackle
61	Jesse Sapolu	left guard	94	Dana Stubblefield	defensive tackle
66	Bart Oates	center	57	Rickey Jackson	defensive end
63	Derrick Deese	right guard	54	Lee Woodall	outside linebacker
79	Harris Barton	right tackle	50	Gary Plummer	middle linebacker
84	Brent Jones	tight end	51	Ken Norton	outside linebacker
80	Jerry Rice	wide receiver	25	Eric Davis	cornerback
8	Steve Young	quarterback	21	Deion Sanders	cornerback
32	Ricky Watters	running back	46	Tim McDonald	strong safety
40	William Floyd	running back	36	Merton Hanks	free safety

Others

4 Doug Brien, kicker; 10 Klaus Wilmsmeyer, punter; 14 Bill Musgrave, quarterback; 18 Elvis Grbac, quarterback; 20 Derek Loville, running back; 22 Tyronne Drakeford, cornerback; 27 Adam Walker, running back; 28 Dana Hall, safety; 35 Dexter Carter, running back; 41 Toi Cook, cornerback; 43 Marc Logan, running back; 55 Kevin Mitchell, linebacker; 64 Ralph Tamm, guard; 67 Chris Dalman, center-guard; 71 Charles Mann, defensive end; 75 Frank Pollack, tackle; 81 Ed McCaffrey, wide receiver; 85 Ted Popson, tight end; 88 Nate Singleton, wide receiver; 90 Darin Jordan, linebacker; 91 Rhett Hall, defensive tackle; 92 Troy Wilson, defensive end; 98 Antonio Goss, linebacker; 99 Tim Harris, defensive end.

FINAL TEAM STATISTICS

	Chargers	49ers		Chargers	49ers
TOTAL FIRST DOWNS	20	28	PASS ATTEMPTS-COMPLETIONS-INT.	55-27-3	38-25-0
by rushing	5	10	Average gain per attempt	5.0	7.7
by passing	14	17			
by penalty	1	1	PUNTS-AVERAGE	4-48.8	5-39.8
			PUNT RETURNS-YARDS	3-1	2-12
TOTAL NET YARDS	354	449	KICKOFF RETURNS-YARDS	8-242	4-48
Total offensive plays	76	73	INTERCEPTIONS-RETURN YARDS	0-0	3-16
Average gain per play	4.7	6.2			
			PENALTIES-YARDS	6-63	3-18
NET YARDS RUSHING	67	133			
Total rushing plays	19	32	FUMBLES-YARDS LOST	1-0	2-0
Average gain per rush	3.5	4.2			
			FIELD GOALS-ATTEMPTS	1-1	0-1
NET YARDS PASSING	287	316			
Sacks-Yards Lost	2-18	3-15	TIME OF POSSESSION	28:29	31:31

FINAL INDIVIDUAL STATISTICS

RUSHING

Chargers: Means 13-33; Harmon 2-10; Jefferson 1-10; Gilbert 1-8; Bieniemy 1-3; Humphries 1-3. Total 19-67.

49ers: S. Young 5-49; Watters 15-47; Floyd 9-32; Rice 1-10; Carter 2-minus 5. Total 32-133.

PASSING

Chargers: Humphries 24-49-2, 275 yards, 1 TD; Gilbert 3-6-1, 30 yards. Total: 27-55-3, 305 yards, 1 TD.

49ers: S. Young 24-36-0, 325 yards, 6 TDs; Musgrave 1-1-0, 6 yards; Grbac 1-0-0. Total: 25-38-0, 331 yards, 6 TDs.

RECEIVING

Chargers: Harmon 8-68; Seay 7-75; Pupunu 4-48; Martin 3-59, 1 TD; Jefferson 2-15; Bieniemy 1-33; Means 1-4; Young 1-3. Total: 27-305, 1 TD.

49ers: Rice 10-149, 3 TDs; Taylor 4-43; Floyd 4-26, 1 TD; Watters 3-61, 2 TDs; Jones 2-41; Popson 1-6; McCaffrey 1-5. Total: 25-331, 6 TDs.

TACKLES (SOLO)

Chargers: Gibson 11 (9); Seau 11 (9); Gordon 5 (5); Mims 5 (5); Griggs 5 (3); Carrington 4 (4); Harper 3 (3); Johnson 2 (2); Lee 2 (2); Richard 2 (1); Clark 1 (1); Davis 1 (1); O'Neal 1 (1); Vanhorse 1 (1). Total: 54.

49ers: McDonald 9 (8); Norton 7 (5); Davis 6 (6); Drakeford 4 (4); Brown 4 (3); Plummer 4 (2); Sanders 4 (2); B. Young 3 (3); Cook 3 (2); Jackson 2 (2); Stubblefield 2 (2); Hall 2 (1); Hanks 2 (1); Harris 2 (1); Mann 1 (1); Woodall 1 (0). Total: 56.

SUPER BOWL RECORDS SET

INDIVIDUAL

GAME

Touchdown passes: 6, Steve Young, 49ers (previous: 5, Joe Montana, 49ers, XXIV)

Highest punting average: 58.8, Bryan Wagner, Chargers (previous: 48.5, Jerrel Wilson, Chiefs, IV)

Kickoff returns: 8, Andre Coleman, Chargers (previous: 7, Stephen Starring, Patriots, XX)

Kickoff return yards: 242, Coleman (previous: 190, Fulton Walker, Miami, XVII)

CAREER

Points: 42, Jerry Rice, 49ers (previous: 24, Rice; Franco Harris, Steelers; Roger Craig, 49ers; Thurman Thomas, Bills)

Touchdowns: 7, Rice (previous: 4, Harris; Craig; Thomas)

Receptions: 28, Rice (previous: 27, Andre Reed, Bills)

Yards receiving: 512, Rice (previous: 364, Lynn Swann, Steelers)

Touchdown receptions: 7, Rice (extends own record)

Combined net yards: 527, Rice (previous: 468, Harris)

TEAM

HISTORICAL

Victories: 5, 49ers (previous: shared with Steelers and Cowboys)

GAME

Points (both teams): 75 (previous: 69 – Cowboys 52, Bills 17, XXVII)

Touchdowns (both teams): 10 (previous: 9, set three times)

Points after touchdown (both teams): 10 (previous: 9, set three times)

Passes attempted (both teams): 93 (previous: 92 – Bills 59 vs. Redskins 33, XXVI)

Touchdown passes: 6, 49ers (previous: 5, 49ers, XXIV)

Kickoff return yardage (both teams): 290, Chargers 242 vs. 49ers 48 (previous: 279, Dolphins 222 vs. Redskins 57, XVII)

WOODFORD PUBLISHING, INC.

660 Market Street, Suite 206
San Francisco, CA 94104
415: 397-1853

Laurence J. Hyman
Publisher and Creative Director

David Lilienstein
Marketing Director

Tony Khing
National Accounts Executive

Jim Santore
Art Director

Kate Hanley
Assistant Editor

Paul Durham
Debbie Fong
Heather Torain
Marketing Assistants

To order
THE OFFICIAL BOOK OF SUPER BOWL XXIX:
The Golden State of Football,
please call
1-800-359-3373.